Control the Conversation

Control the Conversation

HOW TO CHARM, DEFLECT, AND DEFEND YOUR POSITION THROUGH ANY LINE OF QUESTIONING

JAMES O. PYLE and MARYANN KARINCH

This edition first published in 2018 by Career Press, an
imprint of Red Wheel/Weiser, LLC.
With offices at:
65 Parker Street, Suite 7
Newburyport, MA 01950
www.redwheelweiser.com
www.careerpress.com

ISBN: 978-1-63265-143-3
Library of Congress Cataloging-in-Publication Data
available upon request.

Cover design by Kathryn Sky-Peck
Cover photograph © iStock
Interior photos/images by Maryann Karinch
Interior by Lauren Manoy
Typeset in Palatino and Helvetica Neue

Printed in Canada
MAR
10 9 8 7 6 5 4 3 2 1

DEDICATIONS

JAMES O. PYLE

To my mom, Wanda Josephine Pyle of Milton, IL, who before she passed at the age of 85 in 2009, believed in me and did the best she could for me, my brothers, and my sisters as well.

Mom, I hope this dedication puts a little dent in a very big IOU.

MARYANN KARINCH

To my mother, brother, Jim McCormick, and Greg Hartley.

ACKNOWLEDGMENTS

JAMES O. PYLE

For a book about answers, first this question: How do I acknowledge and thank all the people who have trained, mentored, and put up with me in this lifetime? My words are not just my own for they all have contributed to this writing. My voice is not just my own, but it speaks from so many people from so many places, about so many things from five years before rock-and-roll music in 1950 to now, some sixty-eight-plus years later.

In the professional arena, I am grateful to fellow veteran and author Greg Hartley for his work with Maryann and introducing us in 2013.

I am equally amazed and appreciate Maryann for her ability to weave the brightly colored threads of our combined life experiences, professional and personal, into a tapestry so easy to read, assimilate, and alter for the good with this new way to consider questions and responses.

And more personally it has to be said, I could not be the person I am or do what I do without my good wife, Debbie, who supports completely, adjusts accordingly, and carried the weight to keep the family balance during this last winter's write.

A very special thank you to my children Jimmy, Corrie Anna, Sharon Marie, Jamie, and Megan for all the years they listened to learn, questioned to learn, and still listen and still question as they will this latest lesson for life. It was from them, and Megan in particular, where the very seed for this book was planted and took quick root.

MARYANN KARINCH

Here's a question I know you can answer: How much fun is it when someone you enjoy is on the other end of a phone call? Well, I would have to say that's how I felt when Jim Pyle and I had our regular calls to develop this book. Together, we joyfully explored the skill sets associated with responding well to questions and feeling confident in any conversation. I thank him for a productive and gratifying partnership.

Also up-front on the list of people to thank is Greg Hartley. Jim and I wouldn't know each other, and maybe not even understand each other as well, if it weren't for Greg. He has been a mentor extraordinaire! Our relationship as coauthors and as friends has been life changing.

I want to thank my sweetheart, Jim McCormick, for consistent and loving support. He also enjoys testing my skills by expecting complete answers to both easy and tough questions. Of course, I need to say the same thing for my mother and brother: When they ask a question, they want to know the whole story. Thanks to them too!

Thank you also to my dear friend Patti Mengers, an award-winning former staff writer for the *Delaware County Daily Times* in suburban Philadelphia, site of Neumann University, where she now lectures on journalism.

I also want to thank my great friends like Mary Saloschin Hubbard at WBUR in Boston and my PEO sisters in Estes Park as well as colleagues who provided intelligent feedback when I asked things like, "What's the best way to communicate this idea?"

Last, but surely not least, we both want to express appreciation to Michael Pye, Laurie Kelly-Pye, Lauren Manoy, and Gina Schenck of Career Press, as well as the new team supporting us at Red Wheel/Weiser.

CONTENTS

Introduction:
You Can Take This
Skill to the Bank

We make our world significant by the courage of our questions and by the depth of our answers.

—Carl Sagan, *Cosmos*

What do you do when someone asks you a question? If the words "answer it" formed in your head, then you need this book.

Generally speaking, a question is an invitation to a conversation, and like any invitation, the person issuing it has an agenda. Your job in responding to the question is to keep your own agenda central in the conversation. That means you don't just answer the question: You use it to provide the information you want to convey.

We have both done a lot of morning drive-time radio to promote our careers and our books, and it's the land of witty banter and eight-second answers.

Yet, these appearances tend to result in an uptick in sales. We can tell you with confidence: It isn't the mere fact that we opened our mouths on the radio that sold books. It's how we used the eight seconds of airtime to respond to a question.

Notice we said "respond" and not "answer."

One of the first distinctions we make in the book is that *responding* to a question is not necessarily answering it. It's better than that. Your response to any and all questions can pack much more power and meaning into it than a mere answer.

In the book, we start by defining the skill set we will help you develop, namely, giving the best response to a question.

To start, you need to "see into" a question and understand what information the other person wants. We explore four areas of disclosure throughout the book: people, things, places, and time. Although the interrogative tips you off to some extent about what the questioner is after—who, what, when, where, why, how, how much—the interrogative is only part of the question.

Wendy Lea, CEO of Cintrifuse, uses a provocative job interview question that has many layers; it's a great example of a question that requires information beyond the "what" that launches it:

> *What will I only know about you after we've worked together for a year?*[1]

What introduces a "thing" question, but a central focus is people—you and me. There is also a decided emphasis on time; the "thing" can't be known until you and I work together for a year. The concept of "worked together" also suggests proximity. The reference doesn't specify a place, but it does imply closeness.

Even if you give a brief response, your ability to identify the component parts of the question will make it richer.

> *In terms of temperament, I'm an introvert. In that first year, you would get that I enjoy being part of a team, but when I want to churn my creative energy, I go to a private space.*

We aren't saying this is the most ideal response to a challenging question. We are saying that it is more compelling than a bare-bones answer like, "I'm an introvert." It provides an answer to *what*, while it also establishes the time frame, the appreciation for other people, and a place that is significant to the answer, that is, a private space.

An interviewer who is inventive enough to ask this question of a job candidate wants more than, "I'm an introvert."

In Part I of the book, you discover the mechanics of good responses, and get adept at separating questions into good ones and bad ones, easy ones and tough ones. We include a close look at how to listen for and use keywords and how to read and use body language.

In Part II, you see the mechanics in use in various settings that are common to many business environments and social situations. We weave exercises into the material to help you sharpen your new skills.

Please take another look at the Carl Sagan quote that opened this introduction. The "depth of our answers" is part of how we make our world significant. That means that the skills you are about to master are life changing!

EXERCISE

We request that you begin your adventure toward mastery by answering four questions. Write down the answers. You will be asked these questions again at the end of the book—and you will be astonished at how different your responses will be.

- ◇ Where were you on a memorable New Year's Eve?

- ◇ Who is your grandfather on your mother's side?

- ◇ What is your favorite restaurant?

- ◇ How did you celebrate your birthday last year?

We did the same exercise to give you a sense of what we see as baseline answers. For contrast, our responses are included at the end as well.

Where were you on a memorable New Year's Eve?
Jim: The backyard of my house.
Maryann: In bed.

Who is your grandfather on your mother's side?
Jim: William "Stump" Bagby.
Maryann: Michael.

What is your favorite restaurant?
Jim: The Wharf.
Maryann: Seasoned.

How did you celebrate your birthday last year?
Jim: Eating seafood.
Maryann: At Seasoned.

We hope you are ready to turn the page to avoid giving boring answers like that for the rest of your life!

PART I

BUILDING THE
SKILL SET

CHAPTER 1

THE FOUR AREAS OF DISCLOSURE

Providing multidimensional answers to questions creates opportunities for you—opportunities to reveal talents, tell a memorable story, convey unique knowledge. Most importantly, inclusive responses open the door to dialogue. Whether it's a job interview, sales meeting, or a first date, instead of the encounter being a bland question-and-answer session, it's a collaboration. One result: You have at least as much control as the other person does over the conversation.

The four areas of disclosure are people, places, time, and things. When you link your responses to these four areas, you mentally organize information in a way that makes it more complete. Depending on the question, you may naturally focus on one area more than another. The important thing to know is what other types of information you want to make sure the questioner hears.

The four disclosure areas are overtly tied to certain interrogatives:

1. **People:** Who?

2. **Places:** Where?

3. **Things:** What? How?

4. **Time:** When?

The interrogative launches your thinking; however, it should not limit it. For example, people exist in a context (place); take actions (things); and have a yesterday, today, and tomorrow (time). When you infuse your replies with multiple subject areas, you don't just answer a question, you *respond* to it.

CATEGORIES OF RESPONDERS

When you answer questions right now—before you've learned techniques that help you control a conversation—you probably have a dominant style. We put people into four categories based on how they tend to answer questions:

1. Handler

2. Dictator

3. Commentator

4. Evader

Identifying how you tend to respond to questions will help you adapt the techniques and tips

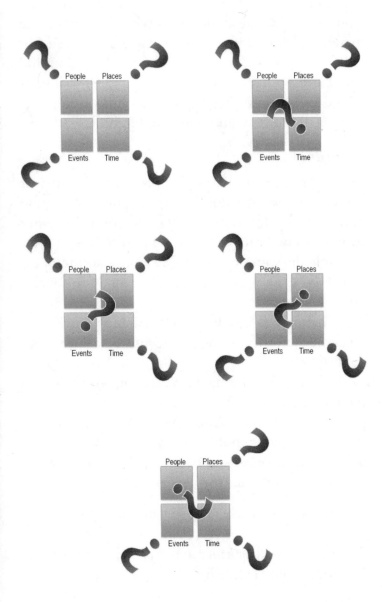

we offer to your own style. If none of these descriptions seems to describe your typical approach to answering questions, share them with a friend or colleague and ask for an assessment. Keep in mind that there are distinct merits to each style, so if your friend calls you a dictator, for example, don't take offense. Build on your style; don't fight it.

Handler

A handler contemplates the best way to answer your question. She might drip a little information and then wait for a comeback to determine whether or not to say more. Another handler trait is to offer multiple answers in a single response so the questioner gets the message that there may be several good answers.

A handler is predisposed to adapt quickly to weaving more than one disclosure area into a response.

Brian was having his first meeting with a potential client for his public relations firm. Dr. S.S. Rodgers's book was just about to be published, and she was interviewing publicists who could likely get her on television. Brian opened with the question, "What are your goals for the campaign?"

Dr. Rodgers: I'd like to be on national television.

Brian: What particular types of shows do you have in mind, Dr. Rodgers?

Dr. Rodgers: To do national shows that women watch and rely on to learn about health issues — although I will say that the same kinds of shows in major markets are appealing.

Brian: What kind of television experience do you have currently?

Dr. Rodgers: It's all local, but I've gotten great feedback. I'm very comfortable in front of the camera and am open to media training if you think that's important to get a national spot.

Brian: Why do you think national television is the best focus for your campaign?

Dr. Rodgers: One of my friends who is a colleague and author has gotten great results from TV exposure. He made the New York Times *bestseller list.*

Brian: If we had a hard time getting a TV spot, how much would a review or article in the New York Times *please you?*

Dr. Rodgers: I think that would be a fabulous springboard to getting some TV exposure.

In this scenario, the handler isn't plagued with uncertainty. Dr. Rodgers feels the need to balance her answers, but she is driving toward a single idea:

She wants a lot of eyes on her. The PR consultant wants to design a program that will hook Dr. Rodgers, and that cannot be done unless it includes broadcast media exposure.

Dictator

We mean nothing pejorative in saying the current president, Donald Trump, comes to mind with this type. A dictator delivers an answer definitively. The negative aspect of a dictator's response is that he has no hesitation about presenting a personal opinion as fact. He may also have a decisive quality to his responses that can be off-putting to people who prefer informed responses over opinions.

A dictator can be extremely good, or extremely bad, at weaving in a number of disclosure areas. The ability depends on what the individual gives weight to and how well that emphasis satisfies the questioner—or the audience on whose behalf the interviewer poses the question, as in the case of journalists.

When asked about the employment status in the "motor car and truck situation" in a January 2, 1942 press conference, President Franklin Delano Roosevelt deftly addressed multiple disclosure areas. Keep in mind that the United States had just declared war on Japan on December 8, 1941, one day after the bombing of Pearl Harbor. Instead of opening his response to a "what" question with a litany of things being done, however, he turned first to people and kept looping back to people. A dictator has a distinct agenda, and that agenda will shape the answer to any question:

> *People will be laid off. Incidentally, the—I have had quite a number of reports from the leaders in labor organization in automobile plants, and they are just about 100 percent in their understanding of the matter, and say that they entirely approve of retooling, and that their people—their members—are willing to be out of work for a little while, if it will aid in the general defense program; it being of course understood that hardship will be taken care of in the meantime, and that they will return to their jobs just as soon as the new tooling comes in.[1]*

Commentator

A commentator is thorough, gives comprehensive answers, and in some cases, he sometimes wades into "too much information" territory. He may provide such a multifaceted answer that it could change the direction of the questioning.

In an interview with Terry Gross for *Fresh Air*, actor Joaquin Phoenix showed commentator tendencies. When Gross asked him about his character in the film *The Master* talking out of the side of his mouth, Phoenix responded:

> *My dad sometimes would talk out of the side; he'd clench down one side of his mouth. And I*

just thought it represented tension in this way, somebody that's just blocked and tight. [2]

Phoenix found the image so compelling that he had a dentist install metal brackets in his mouth. Using rubber bands to force his jaw shut on one side, he tried to replicate his father's speech when his teeth were clenched. Describing this process was just the beginning of a detailed, rambling explanation. He suddenly became aware of his digression and interrupted himself:

If I was driving and I heard this, I'd change the channel . . . I'd be like, "Joaquin, shut up." [3]

This is precisely how someone asking a commentator a question may feel.

On the positive side, a natural commentator has no blocks to bringing multiple subject areas into an answer. The challenge for a commentator is paring the information to keep the response on point.

Evader

A person who sidesteps questions habitually probably just has an idiosyncratic way of listening and processing information; we would call that person an evader. Another version of the evader is someone who feels uncomfortable answering questions for some reason.

Other types of people become evaders when they want to avoid answering because they have something to hide. In legal terms, when someone deliberately gives an evasive answer in the discovery process, it's regarded as a failure to answer, and it's potentially a serious offense. We are not talking about those situations or deliberate prevaricators here.

The typical evader is someone who can frustrate people who are more linear thinkers by simply going off topic. If you ask, "What did you think of that movie?" the person might answer by telling you how the lead actor used to be married to another actor who died tragically, and this movie reminded her of their ill-fated love affair. That's one way of telling you what she thought of the movie, although it's not the angle you had in mind.

A person like this might be a creative problem-solver who comes at challenges from a different perspective than most people. She might be a valued member of her team despite the fact that she exasperates everyone else on it when she answers a question.

An evader might be very comfortable weaving in multiple subject areas in a response, but like the commentator, might struggle to include only the information that has relevance.

Focus on the Four Areas

When you know how to frame information about people, places, things, and time, you will have an easier time integrating it into your responses.

People

Among the many common ways to sort people are physical appearance, culture, personality, religion, nationality, and marital status. The categories are endless if you sort people by what they eat, how they dress, what music they listen to, what language they speak, and whether they are left- or right-handed. All these categories have associated vocabularies to help you describe people.

Many times, the person you will be describing in response to a question is yourself, so having the vocabulary to describe who you are may be the most important set of "people terms" you can integrate.

Give some thought to how you capture your dominant qualities as a professional, a friend, a partner, a visitor to Disneyland. And then, we recommend you consider how one or more of the "ten characteristics of really interesting people" might apply to you and become part of a conversation about you. If you are in a situation like a job interview or a reception at a conference, the value of having terms like these associated with you could go a long way.

These characteristics were identified by cartoonist Jessica Hagy, who readily admits that she has no credentials to say anything about social science! Nonetheless, we think her terms are provocative enough to share. They can help get your juices flowing about how you might talk about yourself. Hagy, whose how-to guide is called *How to Be Interesting*, identifies the characteristics as follows:

1. **Adventurous.** The world outside is always HD, 3D, color, and smellavision.

2. **Generous.** Share what you discover.

3. **Active.** Even the slowest progress is progress forward.

4. **Strange.** Shine a spotlight on your weirdness. Get it insured.

5. **Caring.** If you don't give a damn about anything, nobody's going to give a damn about you.

6. **Humble.** Minimize the swagger. Egos get in the way of ideas.

7. **Daring.** Try and fail, and try a few more times.

8. **Original.** Hop off the bandwagon. Host a shindig of your own.

9. **Brave.** Grow a pair. You need to be ballsy to get it done.

10. **Self-assured.** Ignore the scolds. Boo to those who say, "Sit down. Behave yourself. Keep your head down. Get in line." It's their problem, not yours.[4]

Places

Responses related to places could address directions, location, appearance, layout, or function. Tips to help you communicate place information in an answer:

◇ Use reference points that are familiar to the person.

◇ Recall how the person may have talked about a place and then "speak her language." For example, if she happened to say, "We're moving the offices to a building near the bell tower," then you have a sense she thinks in terms of landmarks. Another person might say, "We're moving the offices to a building uptown and northwest of here."

◇ Communicate scale as accurately as you can. Assuring a customer that the warehouse is full of the desired inventory is different if the warehouse is 2,000 square feet or 10,000 square feet.

◇ Communicate distance as meaningfully as you can. If you're asked at a job interview how much of a commute you would have, and you're coming into Manhattan from New Jersey, putting the answer in terms of the number of subway stops makes more sense than saying you live ten miles away.

A place would commonly start with "where," however, it could be phrased something like, "What's the location of your favorite conference facility?"

When we were developing this book, the importance of providing a complete answer that included a specific place came into play in an unusual way.

Maryann asked Jim about some of his early work experiences. As part of his response, he mentioned that he had worked for Graceland Fairlawn cemetery in Decatur, Illinois. Maryann asked her partner, also named Jim, where his grandparents were buried because she knew they were from Decatur, Illinois. It was the same cemetery, and Jim Pyle was later able to help the other Jim with issues related to the family burial plots there.

Things

Things fall into these categories:

◇ **Mechanical:** A bicycle, a chair, a ballpoint pen

◇ **Electronic:** Computers, mobile phones, fitness trackers

◇ **Structure:** A building, a bridge, the Eiffel Tower

◇ **Process:** Using a spreadsheet, baking a cake, brushing lint off your jacket

◇ **Concept:** Democracy, capitalism, heaven

◇ **Expendable:** Toilet paper, a candy bar, hand sanitizer

Many things combine mechanical, electronic, and expendable aspects, so it is common to get crossover. A car has mechanical parts, electronic components, and expendable pieces, and you could say the same for some buildings.

Keeping these categories in mind, a thing question could be, "How do handle firing someone?"—as in a process or technique—as well as, "What kind of snow blower do you prefer?"

Time

Every event is connected to its past and future, as well as its present. It occurs at a certain moment but also in a context: Something happened before it and something followed it.

If you were investigating a car crash, you would want information to help you construct an entire timeline: the seconds leading up to the crash, the crash itself, and the moments that followed. And you would want to look at that timeline backward and forward to ensure you had all the pieces and they fit together tightly.

For most people, memory tends to be linear; going forward makes sense, but traveling backward in time might be challenging. Yet, there are advantages to practicing that backward approach to a timeline. When pressed to remember things out of sequence or in reverse sequence, our brains tend to work differently. It's possible to recall things we overlooked before.

Questioners often hide information they want about time in a question—and don't even realize it. Instead of the question starting with "When," it might be something like, "How did you manage to get everyone out of the building after the alarm went off?" Your response needs to capture a timeline as well as a process. What you did is only part of the story; what you did *when* is a more complete picture of your accomplishment.

EXERCISE

Many websites offer trivia games and quizzes. Pick one and explore how your ability to weave multiple subject areas into an answer makes the answer much more interesting.

The example we chose is the Bond Quiz—that's James Bond—because we've both seen all the Bond films. Pretend you are also a Bond fan and are at a party. Someone asks you, "What was the name of the first Bond film?" You could just answer, "*Dr. No.*" You win, but you aren't very interesting; you're just a trivia buff. What if you took an extra few seconds to say,

> *Dr. No. in 1962, and the action is in Jamaica. Ursula Andress was the Bond girl—and she showed up again five years later in the funny Bond movie—the first Casino Royale.*

Have fun choosing a trivia category that is your area of expertise and responding to the questions with answers that integrate as many of the subject areas as you can.

Donald Davidson's ability to do this changed his life. Davidson had cultivated an intense interest in the classic motor race known to all as the

Indianapolis 500. Leaving his job as a cinema projectionist in Salisbury, Wilshire, in South West England, he showed up in 1964 with suitcase in hand at the Indianapolis Motor Speedway. After a few hours of talking with race officials and demonstrating his "selective retention" memory of every driver, car, team, manufacturer, and race statistic, he was given full-access credentials and invited to the master control tower of the speedway to talk with Sid Collins, the radio "Voice of the 500." Over the world's largest single-day broadcast radio program, he asked Donald random questions found only in books, archive films, and the collective consciousness of die-hard race fans. In theory, no one person could store so many details and stories about the Indy 500.

At age thirteen, Jim had his ear inclined to a GE clock radio in Southern California, and he can recall that broadcast. Donald Davidson not only answered random questions with a name or a car but also responded with the rich background about teams, engines, tires, fuel combinations, and so on.

Other coannouncers joined in, believing that they may surely ask something he may not know about the speedway's then nearly fifty-year history. It was a unique unscripted questioning event witnessed audibly by millions around the world.

Davidson's warm, factual, and full-spectrum responses earned him a return to the broadcast booth the very next year. What transpired thereafter is a great testimonial to well-phrased responses to questions. Davidson continued living and working with the racing community, holding various positions that culminated in his official designation "Historian of the Indianapolis Motor Speedway," the only person to hold such a position on a full-time basis for any motorsports facility in the world, according to the *2009 Indianapolis 500 Official Program*. Now a member of the Auto Racing Hall of Fame, he is currently still walking the on-site museum in Indianapolis, answering any and all questions.

You don't need a selective retentive gene to answer questions well. Just think beyond the first thing that comes to mind and build from there. When you make it factual whenever necessary and also interesting, you invite a continuation of the conversation, all the while controlling it.

• •

CHAPTER 2

RESPONDING WELL TO EASY QUESTIONS

An easy question is one in which you know who is asking, what is being asked, why the question is being asked, and when the answer is required.

Both easy and tough questions can be classified as good or bad, so we want to start with clarity about what constitutes a good or bad question.

GOOD AND BAD QUESTIONS

Good questions fall into six categories: direct, control, repeat, persistent, summary, and non-pertinent.

Direct

A simple question, generally consisting of one interrogative, one verb, and one noun or pronoun. It's a question like "Who are you?" or "What did you eat for lunch?"

Control

A question designed to test a person more than to discover new information. For example, if you know that someone on your sales team had a disagreement with his colleague Mike, you might ask a control question like, "How did it go with Mike today?" You already have the information; you just want to find out how the person answers it.

Repeat

Two different questions that ask for the same information. If you asked, "How many computers do you have in this department?" the manager you're speaking with might respond, "There are ten." Later on, when you're talking with him about something different, like space requirements, you might ask, "How many cubicles do you have on this floor?" He might respond, "Ten," which is a way of confirming the number of computers in the department. It's not an absolute test, but rather a cross-check.

Persistent

Roughly the same question posed in different ways to extract more complete information. By "persistent," we mean searching for a thorough answer but not being insistent. Persistent questions are useful if you suspect that the person is not being truthful or telling you everything you would like to know. "Where did you go on your vacation?" might elicit the answer, "Santa Fe." Although it's possible that Santa Fe is the only place he went, you might ask, "Did you get to Albuquerque on your vacation?" Persistent questions also help you check out a person's story.

Summary

A question that gives the other person a chance to revisit the answer. It's not meant as a trap, but it's an attempt to clarify: "Did I understand you correctly when you said . . ."

Non-pertinent

A question that is just meant to get someone to open up to you, such as, "How was your drive over here?" The purpose of it is to keep the conversation going without having to think too much; it gives both parties time to decompress and possibly take the conversation in a new direction.

Bad questions fall into four major categories, and even they can sometimes be useful, especially from the point of view of the person being asked the question. A bad question is a poorly structured question; you can sometimes take advantage of the fact that the question is not stated clearly.

Leading

The question supplies an answer and possibly prevents a truthful, accurate answer. "How bad do you feel about getting fired?" is a leading question because it implies the person who got fired feels bad.

In certain contexts, this kind of bad question could work to your advantage.

◇ The HR director asks you a variation of that question in a job interview: "How bad did you feel when your last company fired you?" This is an opening to sound smart and confident: "Pain is a good teacher. I felt bad and then looked forward."

◇ In a meeting with a prospective client, the prospect asks you the leading question, "How concerned are you that your competitor's new product will cut into your sales?" You respond, "Very concerned, and that's why we dropped the price on our current product until our new one is available next quarter."

Negative

Use of a negative word such as *never* or *not* makes it unclear what the person is asking: "Are you never going to not stop trying to get a job that pays $100,000 a year?" This is a badly phrased question—end of story. The best response is to rephrase it to convey your message, "If you're asking me if am still in hot pursuit of a $100,000 a year job, then the answer is yes."

Vague

The information sought is broad or nebulous. For example, a marketing consulting client of yours asks you the following: "Given the rapid developments in technology, our company executives have a lot of opinions about which way to go. What do you think?"

⬦ The downside of a question like this is that you have no firm idea of what information the person seeks. Your answer is guided by extrapolation, that is, you make assumptions of what the person is looking for based on previous conversations and perceptions of that individual's priorities.

⬦ The opportunity with a question like this is that you provide whatever response both suits your purposes and syncs with your extrapolation. If you wanted to interest this marketing client in your company's new big-data solutions, then this is an opening to do that: "I think the time is right to invest in a big-data solution."

Compound

Subjects are combined in the same question, so the person is essentially asking two questions at once. Americans are particularly accustomed to this because journalists who ask questions at White House press conferences and at celebrity events tend to cram as much as possible into one question. Someone new to interviewing job candidates might ask a compound question like, "What did you like most about your last job, and what are you hoping to experience here?"

◇ The downside of the question is that you don't know for sure which part of it holds more interest or weight for the interviewer.

◇ The opportunity is that you can steer the response toward the topic you find more compelling without totally ignoring the other question: "This company has hit a sweet spot with its new product line, and I would be thrilled to promote it. I've always enjoyed promoting great products."

One more type of question would be considered "bad" under certain circumstances. People often ask yes-or-no questions when they want a narrative response. We're calling that a bad question because it doesn't ask what the person really wants to know. Commonly, they will open with

Will you—
Can you—
Do you—
Would you—
Could you—
May I—
or a variation of these.

When someone asks, "Will you marry me?" the clear intent is a one-word response, preferably yes. When someone asks, "Do you see yourself managing the department in five years?" chances are good there is an embedded *why* in that yes-or-no question. That poorly phrased question is your chance to respond with a complete narrative.

EASY QUESTIONS, EASY ANSWERS

To recap how we defined an easy question, it's one in which you know who is asking, what is being asked, why the question is being asked, and when the answer is required. Guidelines for giving the answer fall into both don't and do categories. The first set of don'ts help you determine whether the question is, in fact, easy; those that follow are good guidelines in any situation. Similarly, the do's apply consistently.

General Guidelines: Responding

DON'TS

⋄ Don't assume. "Easy questions" can move into the "tough questions" category.

» The person who is asking the question may or may not be the person who wants or needs the answer. Particularly if you are in a job interview or sales situation, the questioner could be a mouthpiece for the decision-maker. If so, the question goes from "easy" to "tough."

» What is being asked is clear if the direct question is a single subject-verb-pronoun construction with no modifiers. For example, "How have you handled firing someone?" is a straightforward question. In contrast, "How well have you handled firing someone?" is not. The qualitative aspect of the second question ("how _well_") sets an expectation that you will divulge feelings as well as actions. Depending on your circumstances, neither question may be an easy one for you, but the second one is definitely not an easy question.

» The motivation behind a question may be unclear for a couple of reasons. One is that the questioner may not be the person who created the question, as we mentioned previously. Another is that there's a backstory to the question. For example, if your prospective client asks if you will consider a six-month service contract rather than a year-long contract, the question might reflect a bad experience with a year-long contract. When you lack clarity on the motivation behind the question, you face a tough question, not an easy one.

» Sometimes the best answer to a question is not one that you give when the question is asked. The final tip on not assuming that your question is an easy one concerns timing: Take context into consideration—job interview, meeting, live radio show, sales pitch—and be clear on whether or not the questioner needs an immediate response. If not, then determine exactly when it's needed, or reclassify it as a "tough question."

◇ Don't fear the question; listen to it.

◇ Don't respond to the question until you understand it. Ask for clarification if any part of the question confuses you.

◇ Don't be afraid of the silence while you think of your response.

◇ Don't "just" answer any question; instead, try to give the most complete response possible. We define that as a response that covers as many of the four subject areas as possible—people, things, places, events in time.

Dos

◇ Listen with your ears and your eyes. There is more on how to do this in Chapters 7 and 8 in the sections on active listening.

◇ Take time to formulate your answer. There are times, such as those discussed in Chapter 9 on meetings and media, when you have to be relatively quick in responding. In certain situations, "dead air" means you will never be invited back. Even so, there is a way to take time to design your answer, and we explore that throughout the book.

◇ Signal your response. Chapter 7 gets specific about the nature of the signal, which might be a smile or a head tilt. Then again, it might be folded arms that project, "I'm done with this conversation."

Characteristics of an Easy Answer

They are the mirror image of the characteristics of an easy question: Who is responding, what information is being conveyed, how the response satisfies the questioner's want or need for information, and timeliness of response.

Who

Just as the questioner may be the mouthpiece for a decision-maker, you may be the mouthpiece for someone else's thoughts. That takes the answer out of the realm of "easy."

In a job interview, "What is your greatest strength?" is potentially an easy question. You are a project manager and your greatest strength is using a Gantt chart for all its worth. On the other hand, you think that's a boring answer, so you respond with something you heard at a conference about great project management. You no longer have an easy answer.

WHAT

A simple answer can weave a great deal of information into it, but without the adjectives and adverbs that create clutter and add emotion. The project manager who is good with a Gantt chart could respond:

> *Ten years ago, I discovered the value of production control tools like the Gantt chart, and I thank my boss at ABC Company for encouraging me. I know how to put these tools to work.*

That is an easy answer to an easy question. And as a bonus, it's an answer that incorporates things (production tools), people (boss), time (ten years ago), and place (ABC Company).

Just for contrast, here is the easy answer with extraneous adjectives and adverbs—and that makes it messy: "Ten years ago, I discovered the incredible value of production control tools like the Gantt chart, and I thank my awesome boss at ABC Company for doing a super job of encouraging me. I really know how to put these tools to work."

HOW/WHY

In a meeting, your boss asks you an easy question, "What help do you need to finish the product on budget and on time?" Unless you have reason to believe he has a hidden agenda, your easy answer is to tell him who (people), what (thing), when (time), and where (place) you need the help.

WHEN

Not all easy questions will need to be answered immediately, nor should they. As an example, your customer asks you how much it will cost to add ten hours of tech support to her monthly service contract, and the best answer may be as follows:

> *To get you accurate numbers, I need to go back to the office and connect with my team. I'll do that right away. There are a few variables here related to scheduling that I can't address on the spot.*

You deliver a complete answer without delivering a complete answer. In other words, you captured people (team), things (variables related to scheduling), time (right away, scheduling), and place (office, on the spot).

EASY QUESTIONS, TOUGH ANSWERS

Based on the earlier discussion, you most likely have a firm grasp of what constitutes an easy question. We also gave you an inkling of why an answer is tough: It contains something other than a clean fact.

The question about firing is a perfect example. Answering the question of how you fired someone is easy—unless it's tinged with emotion for you.

Asking how well you fired someone is hard because it necessarily involves your judgment of your own behavior.

To make the situation more complicated, perhaps you don't want to admit you ever fired someone because the one time you did it, the company got sued. If you come clean with information on how you fired the person, you immediately get caught in an incriminating statement.

A tough answer is an answer that includes both fact and feeling, *or* it focuses on a fact that you do not want to divulge.

Let's say that you are in line for a promotion—a big promotion. The HR director for your company calls you into a meeting to discuss your future with the company. You are confident you know who is asking the questions, what is being asked, why the questions are being asked, and when the answers are required. That means you face a plateful of easy questions. Put yourself in that conference room and answer each of these questions:

◇ What is your definition of success?

◇ What do you value most?

◇ How do you handle stress?

To what extent did you infuse emotion into any of your responses? You may have honestly answered, "I value my family most of all. I get the greatest joy in life from my children." If you did anything like that example—with any of the three questions—you gave a tough answer to an easy question.

Don't avoid doing that. Just know that you are adding a layer to your response; you are answering an easy question with a tough answer. Expect to have the questioner use that answer as a spade to dig deeper into your thinking and feeling. For example, the follow-up question might be another one the questioner intended to be easy and nonthreatening: "That's beautiful! So how do you manage the balance between work and family?" Unfortunately, for you the answer is tough because you are in the process of divorcing the children's other parent and don't want to bring that fact into the conversation.

EASY QUESTIONS, DEFLECTED ANSWERS

By deflecting, you cause something to change direction. An easy question comes at you, and you use your response like Wonder Woman's cuffs: Bullets ricochet off them. British communications expert Peter Bull studied how British politicians have avoided and deflected questions over the decades.[1] Two of the techniques he documented are:

⬧ **Questioning the question.** You could request more explanation or bounce the question back: "Please tell me more about what you want to know."

⬧ **Providing an incomplete answer.** You move the question away from you by giving a slice of an answer and then moving on to something else.

There are myriad ways to deflect questions; the problem is that many of them make you sound foolish—like pretending you heard the smoke alarm go off in the hallway. The two previously cited techniques at least give you the opportunity to move the question toward something you choose to answer.

EASY QUESTIONS, NO ANSWERS

Say, "I'm sorry, but I don't have an answer to that." Another possibility used often by politicians is, "I don't recall exactly."

Excuse yourself.

In a sales situation, you might say, "I don't have that information with me" or "I'm not privy to that, however, I will ask my boss to call you." In the military, the sentence is, "That's above my pay grade."

Another approach, also used commonly by politicians, is to use terms in the question by repeating it without answering it:

"Congressman, how did that provision on immigration get into the tax bill?"

"I understand you are asking about how that provision on immigration got into the bill and it is an issue that our committee feels is very important to explore."

Unless your intent is to annoy people, avoid nonanswers like that.

Easy Questions Not Worth Answering

There was a time—and hopefully it's long gone—when some companies recommended throwing oddball and brainteaser questions at job candidates. Google was one of those companies, but they gave up the practice because company executives concluded such questions were worthless.

> *We found that brainteasers are a complete waste of time. How many golf balls can you fit into an airplane? How many gas stations in Manhattan? A complete waste of time. They don't predict anything. They serve primarily to make the interviewer feel smart.*[2]

If you have the misfortune to be asked a question like this in any environment except a social one, you might just smile and respond, "I'll get back to you on that one tomorrow."

Or you could take a collaborative approach: "I have no idea, but let's work on that together and see what we come up with."

ANSWERING A QUESTION WITH A QUESTION

There are artful ways to use a question as a response. This is opposed to a mere repetition of the question to buy time, as presidents often due by responding to a reporter with, "Did you mean to ask me . . . ?"

Another useless, and often annoying, comeback is a rhetorical question, that is, a question that theoretically has an obvious answer, so you don't expect an answer. For example, your customer asks you if there is any product on the market that's better than yours. You respond: "You didn't think I would say yes to that, did you?" It's neither funny nor useful.

Questions that serve a function—other than delay and obfuscation—might be classified as *reflective* and *provocative*. The impetus behind a question as a response is:

⬦ to clarify.

⬦ to redirect.

⬦ to drive to a conclusion.

Questions that Clarify

Responding with a question can both clarify what was asked and allow the responder to clarify his own thinking.

REFLECTIVE QUESTIONS

A memorable example of how questions can elucidate the meaning of a response comes from a *Fresh Air* interview that NPR's Terry Gross did with singer-songwriter Ray Charles in 1998. A box set of Charles's country music recordings had just been released, and she asked him why he chose to perform "You Don't Know Me."

> *The songs that I choose start with the lyrics. What are the lyrics saying to me? What kind of story are they telling me?. . . I tell myself, now, how many people will this song fit? I mean, does it sound like most people can relate to it?*[3]

Charles used questions to take us inside his head as he considered whether or not to do a song. In this case, the questions provided answers in a more personal way than declarative sentences could. At the same time, his reflective questions made Terry Gross seem very insightful.

The interview is considered one of the ten best ever done in the more than thirty years Gross has been doing *Fresh Air.* Ray Charles's answer to a simple, well-timed question illustrates how the quality of a question-and-answer exchange comes from the contributions of both participants.

Meetings and job interviews are no different. How you respond to a question can either build momentum and keep it going or bring the moment to a screeching halt. Let's say you are applying for a position as a major gifts officer for an art museum.

The museum director asks you about ways to raise funds for a new wing of the building. You might get more clarity about what the director hopes to hear by responding with reflective questions like these:

> *I start by listening for passion. What are the potential donors saying about their love of art? What makes them thrilled to walk through our doors? Why do they feel proud to come our events? To support you and your vision?*

A logical follow-up from the director might be, "Fascinating! How would that information help you shape your campaign?" This is an opening to let you explore a process rather than list things like, "Black-tie events, offering to put their names on a plaque. . ."

PROVOCATIVE QUESTIONS

Provocative questions can help get clarity using keywords, a topic explored in depth in Chapter 5. They will often be yes-or-no questions that simply pinpoint the topic to be discussed.

For example, your customer asks you, "What's the importance of all these new features in the product upgrade?" You respond with, "Would you like to discuss the new features so that you know exactly what they do?" You spotlight "new features" because that is what you want to cover, and it seems to be what the customer is centered on. It's also possible, though, that the customer is asking in a roundabout way *how* important the new features are, perhaps because he's trying to avoid paying more for the new product. In that case, he gives you a no and admits that he wants to talk about avoiding additional expense.

Regardless of the response—yes or no—you get clarity.

Another way to go is either-or construction. For example, a customer asks you a vague question about upgrades to the software package you provide his company: "What are we looking at regarding those upgrades to the software you and I talked about last year?"

You respond: "Is your primary concern the timing of the upgrades or exactly what they will consist of?" With that question, you pick up the keyword *upgrades* and ask the customer to establish what is more important: when or what.

Another approach to get clarity is to put the emphasis on the part of the question you want to answer: "Is your main interest in what those upgrades are going to do for your daily operations?"

Questions that Redirect

Questions that redirect also require you to spot keywords—so you can avoid using them. The last thing you want to do is reinforce the importance of a topic if you're trying to distance yourself from it.

You may think that question-dodging is an inherently bad thing. You want to keep yourself on the straight-and-narrow path to a response, especially when the question is theoretically an easy one. Based on research done by Harvard Business School professor Michael I. Norton and his colleague Todd Rogers, you may want to rethink that. They looked at the phenomenon of "conversational blindness," that is, not answering the question that was asked, and instead, sidestepping or redirecting it. They found that people tended to value "style over substance,"[4] therefore, hearing someone move to a topic they handled well was preferred to answering a question poorly: "People prefer, trust, and like a question-dodger who is smooth and sounds confident over a question-answerer who is unsmooth and stammers."[5]

REFLECTIVE QUESTIONS

The question posed to you is, "Why are you willing to take a pay cut to work here?" You know you don't want to give the real answer, which is that you exaggerated your previous salary and have now been out of work for two months and are flat broke. You say:

> *How could someone really know what an ideal job is without taking a few chances?*

You have redirected the emphasis from "pay cut" to "ideal job" and associated it with risk-taking—but not your risk-taking. By shifting the pronoun to the third person, you are taking the focus off yourself as well as the proposed topic.

PROVOCATIVE QUESTIONS

During a promotional tour for a new movie, actress Keira Knightley was asked how it's possible to juggle being a married woman and have a career. Without meanness in her voice, Knightley sweetly redirected with: "Are you also asking the men that · today?"[6] This is the kind of sharp retort a person can get away with in a social situation or a media interview, but it would be hard to pull off in a sales meeting or job interview, for example.

By the way, a reflective version of Knightley's answer might be: "How could I be so fortunate to have both? What did I do to deserve such wonderful costars in both aspects of my life?" At that point, in order to move completely off the subject, a comment directing the conversation back to the original point of the meeting or interview could work: "I really am delighted to be part of the team that brought this important project to life." That approach to redirecting is a two-part process: Using question(s) to back away from the original one, and then following immediately with statement that establishes a new topic.

Politicians are sometimes quite good at asking provocative questions in response to a question that makes them squirm. As long as the tone is not accusatory or abrupt, and the body language conveys openness, this approach is easier to pull off than you may think.

In an interview you are asked about a black-tie event you are coordinating to raise money for the local library: "Why aren't you doing something that more of the community can afford to be involved in?" Your artful response is:

> How much is that question rooted in a concern this gala won't raise the $10,000 we believe it will?

A provocative question like that is like a curve ball. As it leaves your mouth, it drops down into territory that the recipient didn't expect, that is, you introduce the fundraising goal of $10,000. Someone skilled in persistent questioning might go back to something like, "But couldn't a community-based event do that too?" One response aimed at further redirection would be another provocative question:

> How would you go about organizing an event for 3,000 people rather than just 100?

QUESTIONS TO DRIVE TO A CONCLUSION

In the context of a negotiation, provocative questions are often valuable tools to driving to a close.

Maryann is a literary agent as well as an author, and she recently had the experience of an editor writing a highly complimentary email about one of her clients. He concluded the email by saying, "When can I see more of the manuscript?" It was a tough question because the author was, in fact, working on the manuscript but wasn't ready to release more of it to anyone. Maryann respond-ed, "We are so pleased you want to see more of the manuscript and wonder when can we expect the contract?" The response was, "Later this week." She asked a specific, results-oriented question.

Reflective questions are not particularly useful in driving to a conclusion. Even in situations where there is likely a power imbalance, such as a job in-terview or sales meeting, provocative questions are the kind of blunt instrument that may serve you well. In Chapter 7, we provide many of the body language clues that tell you the other person is re-ceptive to you and has a sense of truth with you. If you sense that—and only if you sense that—then proceed with a provocative question to move to-ward a close.

A job applicant who is well qualified for a posi-tion requiring unique skills might be appropriate in using a tactic like this:

"Why should we hire you for this position?"

"How difficult is it to find someone who has a background like mine and the strong desire to be part of this company?"

Regardless of the context, realize that anytime you use a provocative question as a response, you need to do it deliberately. This is not the kind of question that should roll out of your mouth because you cannot think of anything else to say.

CHAPTER 3

RESPONDING WELL TO TOUGH QUESTIONS

The first definition of a tough question is an inversion of the definition of an easy one: You have uncertainty about who is asking, what is being asked, why the question is being asked, and when the answer is required. The second definition is that a tough question puts you on the spot. You may have clarity on the who, what, why, and when, but you could go different ways with the response and aren't sure which way is best. Like easy questions, tough ones can be classified as good or bad.

TOUGH QUESTIONS, EASY ANSWERS

Parsing is a way to create an answer easily to a question that involves factors such as emotion, long-term memory, and/or analysis—all of which complicate a question.

"Who had a life-changing influence on you when you were sixteen years old?" Despite its simplicity, this question has the potential to be tough, because it forces you to do mental maneuvering, to move back in time, and to remember your priorities at that moment in time. If you parse it—that is, break it down into its parts—you can make it easy by recognizing it as a people, thing, and time question.

In parsing it, put the easiest piece first: time. You think about being sixteen again.

The next piece is the "thing" component. Determine what really important decision or event occurred when you were sixteen.

After that, the answer to "who" will come to you.

In milliseconds, your head races through big decisions you made when you were sixteen. "Take Sarah to the prom" pops into your head, but that's probably only relevant if you married Sarah. In other words, don't necessarily say the first thing or person that occurs to you. Breathe; think about how a decision you made at sixteen fits into the big picture of your life before you decide how to answer the question.

You have fleeting thoughts that you decided to go to college, join the Marine Corps, marry Sarah, quit the basketball team, and become an astronaut. You only acted on one of those decisions: Go to college.

You have arrived at the easy answer: One person had a huge influence on your choice of going to college: the teacher who encouraged you to become a writer. Following this logic tree to the end, you can probably respond in under five seconds that the person who had a life-changing influence on you when you were sixteen was your high school English teacher.

It's an easy answer to a tough question, unless you let the question strangle your thought process.

All you had to do was:

1. Identify the subject areas in the question.

2. Put them in order from easy to hard, in this case, time, thing, and person.

Imagine you are interviewing for a sales rep position and you get this question: "What is your sales process?" It's tough because it comes across as an obvious "thing" question; it's about your process. Embedded in it are questions about people and time, however. In this case, the "thing" may be the easiest part to address. With that in mind, a possible answer is:

My process centers on building rapport with the prospect, and I start doing that from the moment I meet the person.

It's an easy answer that moves from thing to people to time.

Tough Questions, Tough Answers

We define a tough answer as one that makes you *and* the questioner think. The first step to responding is probably going to be buying yourself some time. If the question is well phrased, you could say, "I like that question!" as a positive start to taking a few breaths and tilting your head as you search for an answer.

Before you start talking, determine which of these techniques might serve you best:

⬦ Tweaking the question to make it clearer if the question is not well phrased.

⬦ Building the answer from nothing, also known as making stone soup.

⬦ Using paradox thinking to address a tough question about your choices.

Tweaking

In Chapter 2, we introduced you to good and bad questions. Even smart people often ask bad questions, phrased so that it's unnecessarily difficult for a respondent to know what's being asked. If someone in a meeting, interview, or sales situation, for example, has just asked you a leading, compound, vague, or negative question, your first response is to clean it up—tweak it into a good question.

You can take all or some of these approaches:

◇ **Ask the person to repeat the question.**
Sometimes, what comes out of the mouth
is not what the brain intended. Give the
person the benefit of the doubt, and hope
that the question will be cleaned up the
second time around.

◇ **Request clarification, focusing on the
subject area that you understood the
least.** For example, the question you hear
is, "How can we get those monthly payments to be more manageable if we play
around with the length of the contract
and maybe add a few features down
the road?" The information you need to
be helpful relates to actions that affect
monthly payments. The question you can
ask is, "Do you want to know what ad-
justments we can make in the length of
the contract and product features to re-
duce the monthly payment?"

◇ **Make sure you are using the same vocabulary.** Using the same rambling question in the aforementioned example, you
need to know what constitutes "manageable" in the customer's mind. Instead of,
or in addition to, restating the question to
clarify, you could just ask, "What do you
consider manageable?"

◇ **Define vague or indefinite terms your
own way, and then answer your version
of the question.** Again, using the previous question as an example, you could

say to the customer: "If you mean how much we must lengthen the contract period and what product features we must remove to get your monthly payment below \$5,000, then here's the answer . . ."

Stone Soup

The folktale of stone soup centers on a little town visited by hungry strangers. No one offers them food, so they take the large iron pot they have with them and fill it with water from the stream. They then place it on a small fire and with great flourish visible to passersby, they place a stone in the water. One dips his ladle into the water and says, "Mmm! Delicious, but it would be so much better if I had a few carrots." Thinking that she would be offered some of the fine soup, a woman gives the travelers a handful of carrots. Similarly, someone else brings a cabbage, and so on. The villagers collect around the pot as the travelers stir the contents and say that the soup just needs a few more things to reach its full potential. Eventually, they have a pot of delicious soup, which they share with everyone.

This is how you build something from nothing and everyone marvels at the result.

Let's say that your tough question is in the context of your job interview for a public relations position for an aviation company. You were prepared for product related questions, personnel questions, financial questions, branding questions—but not this: "How would you handle crisis management if one of our aircraft crashed into a mountainside and a United States senator was killed?"

You face a "thing" question that involves time-sensitive action and an important person, with "place" playing a significant role in the story.

You put your stone in the pot of water: "As we learned from Johnson & Johnson, a good outcome from an experience like this strengthens a company's reputation for years to come." So far, you've done nothing to make the soup except suggest that you know what good soup tastes like. The reference to Johnson & Johnson is a classic crisis PR victory. After seven people in the Chicago area died from ingesting Tylenol capsules containing cyanide, the company got out in front of the crisis and immediately pulled all its of product nationwide—31 million bottles of Tylenol.

The person who posed the question nods knowingly. "Yes, I think one of the first things the CEO did was get out there and tell people what happened." Now you have carrots.

The comment provides an opportunity to ask a question, "How fast would your CEO respond to the tragic news?" The answer gives you the cabbage.

The interactive process has the potential to give you the information to build your answer in a way that reflects company policy, procedures, and priorities. Keep stirring as you add each new ingredient and soon, voilà, great soup.

PARADOX THINKING

In meetings and interviews, a common type of tough question involves a choice between options. For example, you are being interviewed for a management position, and the interviewer wants to know how you might handle a project that either can't come in on budget or can't come in on time if it's going to hit the mark on quality. This is a time for *paradox thinking*, a term that Deborah Schroeder-Saulnier introduced into popular use with her book *The Power of Paradox*.

> *Paradox thinking is "and" thinking. It is thinking that identifies pairs of opposites and determines how they are interdependent relative to a key goal . . .*

> *Paradox thinking enables balanced management of conflicting objectives. A company wants to be known for innovation at the same time customers embrace it for its stability, to thrill shareholders with strong short-term revenue results and concurrently take actions to ensure long-term health. From those two examples alone, it should be easy to see how failure to manage a critical pair of opposites results in the company stumbling and, perhaps, failing.*

Adopting an appreciation for paradox ends the practice of viewing conflicting needs separately and addressing one over the other.[1]

The goal implied in the project management question is quality. The conflicting needs are money and time. Without having more specifics on the amount of money or length of time relative to the scope of the project and desired outcome, you can't give a specific answer to how you would handle this—but you can give a thought-provoking answer. If you assert confidently that this is an opportunity to consider time and budget as interdependent factors rather than either-or, you start the questioner down *your* intelligent way of approaching the challenge. You might begin by pointing out that an either-or choice in a project often leads to results like the Leaning Tower of Pisa and the Tacoma Narrows Bridge.

Paradox thinking came into play with a human resources consultant we know; this situation happened years before the term was coined. A trade group in Washington, DC, had a terrible personnel situation in one of its departments. The department head was beloved by members of the board and hated by her staff. The staff displayed arrogance and disrespect in response to what they saw as arrogance and disrespect shown to them.

The organization's president saw this as an either-or: Either keep the staff intact and fire the department head, or fire the staff and keep the department head. That is how the president posed the question to the consultant: "Which option should we take—fire her or fire them?"

After doing interviews with all the people, the consultant responded, "Keep her and keep them."

"How's that going to work?" The president probably figured he had just wasted his money on this consultant.

She told him that her interviews indicated that Kate, one of the staff members, was an extremely good communicator and could be trained as a go-between. Her job would be to ensure the flow of work and information back and forth between the boss and the staff. In a matter of weeks, the new system functioned well. The unexpected benefit was that the way Kate expressed her boss's thoughts and orders made the boss seem more pleasant to the staff. Their anger dissipated. The same could be said for the department head; she was getting a warmer feeling about the dedication and competence of the staff because of the way Kate communicated their results.

The big take-away with this story and the application of paradox thinking is that you should consider how balanced and intelligent you can sound when you respond to an either-or question by saying "and."

Tough Questions, Deflected Answers

We have classic political wisdom to open this discussion. After a debate between president Barack Obama and presidential candidate Mitt Romney, the latter caught criticism from a reporter over an evasive answer. Romney responded, "You get to ask the questions you like. I get to give the answers I like."[2]

Sometimes, interviewers and customers ask inappropriate or ill-timed questions, or at least they are perceived as such by the person on the other end of the question. A pop culture example—a faux pas that dented the ratings of the interviewer—is the question-and-answer between Oscar-winning actress Jane Fonda and NBC's Megyn Kelly. Theoretically, the soft-news morning program was supposed to focus on Fonda's new movie; instead, Kelly asked her about her plastic surgery. Fonda deflected by verbally wagging a finger at Kelly, indicating that she was out of line.

It is not likely that in any professional situation you will be in a position to finger wag. We will show you other ways to get the job done. In other words, we'll prove how right Mitt Romney can be.

First, we have to issue a warning: Many people will blush and/or fidget when asked a question that makes them uncomfortable. You can control the fidgeting by stopping yourself from pulling on your ear, rubbing your fingers together, or doing the nervous gesture you usually do. If you tend to blush, however, then you will probably blush. Take a few breaths and use one of the deflection techniques described here to shift the questioner's attention to what you are saying. You can blush and display a confident presence at the same time if you sit up straight and speak in complete sentences.

Storytelling

"Why did you leave your last job?" could be a perfectly innocent question, not intended to trap you in any way. The straight answer is, "On paper, I was laid off, but I was actually fired." You decide against blatant honesty; you've only been in this job interview for five minutes, and that information might sour the interviewer's impression of you. You could say:

> *My manager walked over to my desk and said, "Hi! How are you?" I knew something was wrong because he had to fly 2,000 miles to be at my desk since he was based in San Jose and I was here in Chicago. He explained that the company had suffered some losses and needed to cut back on staff at various branch offices. "Here it comes," I thought. And with that, I found myself with a very nice severance package.*

Natural storytellers will sometimes deflect without even meaning to. They are entertaining, drawing the listener away from one world and into another. As long as a story is apropos and succinct, it has a place in nearly every business encounter. Paul Smith has written two bestselling business books about the value of storytelling in a professional environment—*Lead with a Story* and *Sell with a Story*. In the latter book, he gives ten reasons why people in sales should use stories as a way to capture attention, build trust, and close a deal.

In the context of a questioning session, whether it's in a sales meeting, job interview, media interview, or any other question-and-answer encounter, these five reasons of Smith's are great reminders that stories can help you put the attention on the point *you* want to make. They help you take control of the conversation.

1. Stories help build strong relationships, especially when a story "provides a personal, intimate, and perhaps vulnerable glimpse into your world."[3]

2. Storytelling speaks to the part of the brain where decisions are made.

3. Storytelling highlights your main idea by moving it to another context.

4. Stories are contagious.

5. Storytelling gives you an opportunity to be original.

Making Connections

In 1929, Hungarian author Frigyes Karinthy hy-
pothesized that everyone in the world can be connected in six steps for fewer. The game of trying to
prove it is called Six Degrees of Separation, and the
pop culture spinoff is known as the Kevin Bacon
Game. If you have the kind of brain that makes connections easily, then you might be well suited to respond to a tough question by doing a six-degrees
kind of maneuver.

Instead of making the connections with people,
however, you're going to do it with topics.

Let's imagine you've arrived for a meeting
with an important prospective client and your colleague—the one with the PowerPoint presentation—is running late. The prospect is trying to make
small talk and ends up asking you, "What movies
have you seen lately?" Seems like an innocuous
question, except that you know your taste in movies
is sophomoric, and if you admit to seeing *Sex Lives
of the Potato Men* for the fourth time, you will have
zero credibility with this person. You would much
rather talk about baseball, which is something you
happen to know a lot about. The exchange might go
like this:

"What movies have you seen lately?"

"It was something about food . . ."

"Oh, I think my favorite food movie is *Julie & Julia!*
Have you seen that?"

You take a shot in the dark because you hav-
en't seen it: "Is that the one that takes place in New

York?" Since hundreds of movies are filmed in New York every year, you have a decent shot at being right.

"Yes—well, the Julie part, anyway."

"Oh, of course. I tend to remember movies made in New York better than a lot of others because I'm such a big Mets fan."

You did it. You just went from movies to baseball in three steps. As long as your prospect isn't a Yankees fan, you've deflected well.

Interpreting

A question with several subject areas gives you an opening to focus on one more than another, or perhaps to ignore a disconcerting topic completely.

You just arrived for a dreaded debriefing session with your boss. The meeting you had yesterday with a top client went off track, and you'd rather have time to do damage control than explain the current situation to a company vice president. Her opening comment and question are: "I hear things were a little rocky at the meeting yesterday. What was all that talk of pulling out of the contract and going with the competitor, and how can we fix it?"

You have already given considerable thought to the "fix it" part, and that is where you will put 100 percent of your energy. As long as the meeting lasts, you will stay away from "all that talk."

Another approach to interpreting a tough question is to focus on a single word. The vice president asks a follow-up question a few minutes later:

"What did you pick up about the client's level of interest in going with the competitor?" You home in on the word "interest." The client has an interest in higher brand recognition more than anything. The client has an interest in celebrity endorsements—and so on.

Discussing

A tough question can be an interviewer's or customer's way of starting a dialogue. Even if the circumstance is a job interview or a contract negotiation, it's possible that the question needs to be heard by you as an entrée to dialog.

The person interviewing you for a management position might look you straight in the eyes and ask, "Why are we still stuck on the triple constraints in project management?" That may or may not be a question, but it certainly gives you an indication that the classic triple constraints you have abided by your entire career may not be revered by this individual.

By commenting, "There are many constraints that can come in play," you don't answer "why," but you do set up a conversation that may give you insights into what this person is thinking.

Channeling

You have to field a big-picture question, but you don't know where to begin or end. Rather than embarrass yourself by being nebulous about certain aspects of the topic, you narrow it to an area of familiarity and expertise.

"Why are you qualified for a management job at this resort?" could take you in any number of directions, from describing your Myers–Briggs profile to spotlighting the value of your MBA education.

> *My work at the ad agency carried huge responsibilities, but the experience that most aligns with your needs here is the two years I managed the student center while doing full-time graduate work. I had to be organized, motivate people, and get myself all over campus on time.*

All of the strategies we described in the section require you to dive into the deep end of the pool and swim like a pro. You can't act squeamish or start treading water and gasping for air. You are in charge of taking the conversation where you want it to go.

Tough Questions, No Answers

A head of state may get away with responding to a tough question with, "We'll have a major announcement on that next week." You can't. The primary way a regular person in a meeting or interview can avoid answering a question is by doing one of the following:

◇ **Be honest.** "I can't give you a good answer to that because . . ." This would be followed by something like "I don't know," "I would embarrass myself with the answer," or "I'd need more time than I have here to think about the most appropriate way to answer that."

◇ **Change the subject.** "Pardon me, but that question reminded me of something I wanted to be sure to tell you at this meeting."

◇ **Excuse yourself.** "Please excuse me for just a moment. Where is your restroom?"

◇ **Do an inversion.** "You asked me about my worst nightmare ever on the job. I get it! But first I'd like to share a short story about a dream come true."

EXERCISES

All three exercises that follow are interactive. You can't get good at them unless you involve other people—preferably people who want to develop the same skill sets that you do.

The first two exercises focus on two of the most useful abilities you can cultivate to control a conversation: storytelling and building connections. People who are facile with either or both can move others in a completely different conversational direction within minutes—if not sooner.

The third exercise invites you to respond to somewhat odd questions—questions that are really used in job interviews, according to Glassdoor,

Quora, Vault, and FlexJobs—with either reflective or provocative questions.

Develop a "What I Do" Story

Paul Smith makes this recommendation in *Sell With a Story* and to his basic suggestion, we want to add that your story should be about 100 words. The point is to arouse curiosity immediately about who you are and what you do. Here's an example from Mark Satterfield in his book *Unique Sales Stories* that tells the "what I do" story of someone in the chicken business:

> *How do you get the chicken from the farm to the retail store, in less than three days, all ready for cooking and smelling nice? That process has a lot of moving parts, a lot of people involved, actually a lot of different companies, and if one thing breaks down from farm to grocery store, the whole thing turns into an enormous, foul-smelling hairball real quickly. So basically what I do is to look at all the steps in the process and try to figure out if there is some way we can do them faster, better, less expensively, or more efficiently.*[4]

Once you develop your "what I do" story, try it out on a few people. If you are an extrovert, you will try it out with people you've just met who ask you about yourself.

Play Six Degrees of Separation, AKA the Kevin Bacon Game

Regardless of whether you are in a conference room with coffee and whole-grain cookies or at a bar with your friends, you will hone your skills by playing this game.

Select a topic by going to a news site online. It doesn't matter which one, but for setup purposes, let's say it's *Huffington Post*. You chose the top news story, and your topic is "earthquakes."

A friend/colleague chooses another topic by going to an entertainment news source. Again, it doesn't matter which one. Your friend's source is *Entertainment Tonight*, and the topic is "Jennifer Aniston." You know the topics, but the person you are playing the game with does not.

Your challenge, without the other friend/colleague knowing what's going on, is to go from earthquakes to Jennifer Aniston in no more than six exchanges in your conversation. For example:

Mexico keeps getting hit with these terrible earthquakes!

Yes! This one wasn't far from Baja, I think.

That's only about an hour from Los Angeles.

Good heavens, I wonder if celebrities will get involved in relief efforts since it's so close to home for a lot of them?

I bet they will. Remember all the stars who were raising money after the Haiti earthquake.

I do! I remember seeing that thing on TV with all those A-listers taking calls.

Yeah, it was amazing. There was Jennifer Aniston answering a pledge phone.

Earthquakes to Aniston in six steps.

Quest for a Question

Fast Company collected unusual interview questions from Glassdoor, Quora, Vault, and FlexJobs for an article entitled "36 Interview Questions That Are Actually Fun to Answer."[5] We are rather sure that not everyone would think they are fun, however, and think that some of them could be better met with a question than an answer. We challenge you to try as a way to become more adept at using questions as a response to tough questions.

For example, you are asked, "You're a new addition to the crayon box. What color would you be?" Your reflective answer could be:

How would I see myself on a Saturday evening as opposed to a Monday morning? How much is the color affected by whether or not I've had a good breakfast? Am I a different color when I feel appreciated than when I feel rejected?

A few other questions to answer with either a reflective or provocative question are:

◇ If you could be any animal in the world, what animal would you be and why? (Quora)

◇ What do you want to be when you grow up? (FlexJobs)

◇ What inspires you? (Vault)

◇ If you were to get rid of one state in the United States, which would it be? (Glassdoor)

◇ Who would win a fight between Spiderman and Batman? (Glassdoor)

CHAPTER 4

THE MOTIVATION BEHIND THE QUESTION

For many years, Maslow's hierarchy of needs theory was used to explain human motivation. In a 1943 paper entitled "A Theory of Human Motivation," Abraham Maslow supposedly theorized that people were motivated first and foremost to fulfill their most basic physical needs for things like food and shelter. Once those needs were met, they would address safety and security. Only after that would they be in a position to work on the desire for social belonging and connection. Having fulfilled that, they could then move to addressing the need for self-esteem and, finally, self-actualization, that is, realizing their full potential as people.

We say "supposedly theorized" because a rigid structure of understanding human motivation is often attributed to Maslow, and it shouldn't be. He didn't exactly say what many people said he did. He talked about the role of values and individual appetites, among other factors, in establishing motivation as well as basic needs.

How does all this humanistic and behavioral theory aid your understanding of why people are asking you questions? Because it's easy to make assumptions about why people are motivated to ask you questions—and those suppositions can undermine you.

In a professional situation, one assumption in the back of your mind may be that the customer or job interviewer is asking you questions because he must. It's his job to get certain information from you. "Safety and security" then become prime motivators: If he doesn't ask you the right questions and get the desired answers, he might lose of the security of his job.

That may be the case in some situations, and when it is, there isn't any real interest in how you think, what stories you tell, or how personable you are. You might as well be an android like Data on *Star Trek Next Generation*—a silicon-based being programmed to provide answers. People who ask questions because they must want nothing more than a *functional relationship*.

We don't think this need for security is the most common motivator, however. Considering that values and personal interests play a role in our motivations—even according to Maslow—we think that most questions are an invitation to connect.

People who ask questions because they see them as a tool to get to know you, as well as discover information, want a *substantial relationship*, not merely a functional one.

SUBSTANTIAL RELATIONSHIPS

Giving Maslow credit for keen insights into human need, we might assert that people who want to have a substantial relationship with you are curious about how your values, skills, interests, and priorities match up with theirs and/or their company's. There is a desire to connect with you for a reason other than keeping a job, and that reason might have to do with social belonging, self-esteem, or even self-actualization.

Whether you are selling something, interviewing for a job, in a meeting, or providing information for an article or broadcast, you are seen as one or more of the following:

1. A source of facts that the person might be able to get from multiple sources but enjoys getting from you.

2. A person who has something in common with the questioner like a goal, an agenda, a mission, politics, religion, or a passion for sports cars.

3. A deep pool of wisdom or knowledge that might help him grow and improve.

4. An individual with huge potential who is worth nurturing and helping to discover opportunities.

There are other variations on these themes with the bottom line being that you are not ever perceived as an android like Data. You have far more to offer the questioner than facts. The general motivation is connection; the specific motivation relates to *what kind* of connection.

To answer that, we will return to the simplistic view of Maslow's hierarchy of needs and use it as a framework for discussion. As part of that discussion, we'll look at how each approach to connecting has potential pitfalls that can "steal" the conversation from you, and we offer tips to augment your control.

Belonging

Four types of questions could indicate that the person you are meeting with wants the relationship to include compatibility. There is a desire for a certain comfort level that allows for easy interaction. You will probably be asked:

NON-PERTINENT QUESTIONS (QUESTIONS THAT AREN'T RELATED TO THE BUSINESS AT HAND TEND TO PUT PEOPLE AT EASE)

Generally, chatting a little about topics of common interest support the kind of bonding that makes it more enjoyable to conduct business. "How was your flight?" is a common opener. Some people use chitchat to avoid talking business, though. If you're in a meeting trying to get something accomplished, use the skill you developed playing Six Degrees of Separation to move back to a work-related topic. For example, the person you are meeting with wants to talk about the heavy snowfall, but you're supposed to walk out of the meeting with a project budget. You might be able to make a leap like, "I hate running numbers about as much as I hate shoveling snow, but we have to do it!"

QUESTIONS THAT INVOLVE A QUID PRO QUO

Divulging a fact that seems personal is a method some people use get others to open up. They figure that giving you a "secret" means that you will respond in kind. "I get really frustrated with people who dash off an email without putting any thought into it. How about you?"

Handled well, the quid pro quo tactic supports a stronger connection. It's part of the standard repertoire of elicitation techniques that spies and interrogators use. (More on that later in this chapter.) We caution you here that, regardless of what is revealed to you, do not respond in kind if the information is sensitive or personal. Control slips away from you quickly if you reveal something that is private or confidential.

QUESTIONS ASKING FOR OPINION RATHER THAN FACT

People who are genuinely interested in your opinion respect your knowledge or expertise enough to appreciate it. They think they will benefit from hearing your views. Unless you know someone well, however, offering an extreme opinion makes you vulnerable in the conversation. It's one more way to lose control. Scholastic, which publishes books and educational materials, has a website with components for teachers, parents, students, and others involved in the educational system. They offer a list of "opinion clues"[1] that we think is a good list of words to avoid when offering your opinion in a professional setting:

◇ Always/Never

◇ Awful/Wonderful

◇ Beautiful/Ugly

◇ Better/Best/Worst

◇ Delicious/Disgusting

◇ Definitely

◇ Enjoyable/Horrible

◇ Favorite

◇ For/Against

◇ Good/Bad

◇ Inferior/Superior

◇ Oppose/Support

◇ Terrible

◇ Unfair

◇ Worthwhile

QUESTIONS ABOUT CHOICES

"Why" questions often engage people in explaining their decision process, and that provides insights into their priorities: "Why did you choose the University of Colorado for graduate school instead of staying at Stanford?"

You can reveal important information about your logic, primary concerns, and agenda with a thoughtful answer to these kinds of why questions. They can also take you down a rabbit hole, however. If the example question occurs during a meeting with a new client or a job interview, you want to stay away from sordid details like your fiancé at Stanford running off with your best friend.

Identify all these types of questions as signals that the questioner is exploring a connection with you. Be conscious of that as a goal of the meeting or interview without letting it overtake the encounter.

Esteem

Someone who sees your presence and contributions as ways to build self-esteem will question you about your accomplishments and your shortcomings. A manager who is considering hiring you wants assurances that you will make her look good. A customer evaluating your product hopes for guarantees that you, your company, and your product will perform better than the competition.

We know a consultant who was flown to Taipei, Taiwan, for a week-long series of interviews with board members of an international technology organization.

Expecting mostly questions about how she planned to address their financial challenges, she was caught a bit off guard by the detailed questions related to her work with other clients. She eventually realized that the board members felt their personal reputations were linked to her turning around the organization's deficit situation—but they were not interested in speculation about how that would happen. They were all technical people with an orientation toward documented accomplishments rather than projection about how expertise could be applied to their problems. Had she realized that sooner in the process, she might have gotten the contract.

Sometimes without even realizing what's happening, people recognize the motivation of the questioner and try to exploit it. Exaggerating accomplishments, bypassing shortcomings, over-promising results—these are the traps people create for themselves. They raise suspicions, possibly having the opposite effect of what was intended.

Keep in mind that someone questioning you with a self-esteem motivation has to know she can trust you. Every overstatement potentially pushes you down a slippery slope of lies and out the door.

Self-Actualization

In *Body Language Sales Secrets*, Jim McCormick examines the needs and desires of people who are considering sizable donations to a charity. These are all related to self-actualization and include reasons that are practical, moral, social, spiritual, and historical.[2]

You will hear questions related to legacy and affiliation, for example, when the person's motivation is
self-actualization, whether the conversation is about
a major contribution or a major purchase.

"Major" is not necessarily defined by a dollar
amount, either. When Jim Pyle was selling plots
in Forest Lawn Memorial Park, he engendered
thoughts about legacy by focusing on what the decision to buy would signify to children and grand-
children. And because Forest Lawn is the final rest-
ing place for so many celebrities since the early
1900s, the sense of affiliation with them is a selling
point. A question such as, "How close will I be to
Walt Disney?" would be relevant to some buyers.

Maryann encountered a physician who hired a
publicist to help him promote lifestyle changes. It
wasn't that he wanted to be famous; he wanted his
insights and discoveries to become part of popular conversation to help people improve their lives.
In interviewing people for the publicity position,
the doctor asked a lot of affiliation questions such
as "Who inspires you?" and "Who has been your
greatest teacher?" The doctor wanted to be sure that
the person who would help him in his trek toward
self-actualization was more likely to read Eckhart
Tolle than Stephen King (although we know plenty of
people who would put Stephen King on a pedestal).

If you are in the relatively unusual situation of
fielding questions shaped by self-actualization concerns, one of the best things to do may be to ask

questions in response. Get clarity on how the person defines legacy, for example, and what kind of people he wants to be associated with.

THEIR MOTIVATION VERSUS YOURS

When there is a mismatch between your motivation in an encounter and the other person's, you can very easily lose control of the conversation. You're basically working at odds.

In some cases, people interview for a job for which they are well suited, and they don't care what the environment is or who else works there. They want a functional relationship and nothing more. We heard from one senior manager in a small New York office that applicants are told people from the office get together occasionally at the bar across the street. "How do you feel about that?" she'd ask them. Usually, that was welcome news, but in one case, an applicant said, "I'm a single mom with three kids. This may not be the best fit for me."

Probably just as often, the reverse is the case. Right out of college, Maryann interviewed for a job with a financial services company. That was probably one of her worst ideas given that the nature of the work was highly impersonal. The manager who interviewed her was looking for a functional relationship and realized after fifteen minutes of questioning that Maryann should walk out the door. The essence of his message was that she liked interacting with people too much to do a job like this. It was a valuable lesson, and to this day, she is grateful for verbally booting her out of the office.

And then there are the miscues that send both parties scrambling to figure out what the other means. We've seen this many times over through the years. Whether it's an office holiday party or a reception at a professional conference, questions that suggest a desire to connect tumble out of someone who's still savoring that last sip of Chardonnay. It's still a work environment, and you're better off following the same guidelines on answering as though you were in a meeting.

Countering Uncertainty

In any situation where the motivation is uncertain, your skill set needs to include maneuvers to determine what it is. Three elicitation techniques used by people in the intelligence community are *quid pro quo*, being deferential, and active listening. Elicitation is generally defined as psychological techniques to get people to talk to you about sensitive subjects.

As we previously noted, when you hear the questioner introduce quid pro quo, it's a sign that he wants to connect with you. You are being set up to exchange like-for-like information. You can initiate it as a way of exhibiting trust, and even a little vulnerability. The other person's response may give you a better sense of whether he is leaning toward a substantial relationship or a functional one. For example, the product you are discussing has a distinctive red color—part of its brand identity—but you might admit that the engineers who designed it had painted it black and no one paid attention to it. Instead of engaging in some give-and-take conversation, the customer moves on to how much it costs. You are going toward a functional relationship, not a substantial one.

Being deferential to the other person's expertise is an invitation to get her to talk—about herself. For example, halfway into your meeting, you hear a question that puts you on the spot and seems to bely your presumption that the person respects you and is motivated to bond professionally. She seems to challenge you with, "What kind of mistakes led to that project failure?"

"You may be in a much better position to assess that than I am," you respond. "Your work on the Acme building is a case study in success, so I'm guessing you have a better grasp of what mistakes kill a project than I do!"

Active listening is a technique covered in Chapter 5 and described more fully in Chapter 6. For now, let's just say that most people love the sound of their own voice. If you ask a question and keep nodding and doing other gestures that display your interest in the response, you encourage the person to keep talking. Listen—endlessly—and make discoveries.

EXERCISE

When you are in an environment where you are certain that people want to connect with you—something low-key and social—pay attention to the kinds of questions people ask you. The black-and-white contrast to these kinds of questions are the ones from someone more interested in a functional relationship than a substantial one.

CHAPTER 5

· ·

ANSWER ENHANCERS

Keywords and body language are the two primary answer enhancers. It's important to look at both of them from the "reading" and the "using" perspective. You spot keywords in the question as well as introduce keywords into the answer; you read the questioner's body language and use your own to reinforce your message.

IDENTIFYING KEYWORDS

In the context of search engine optimization, "keyword" has a definition that is more specific than ours. In the broadest sense of the concept, keywords serve as a key to understanding the meaning of something that has been expressed. They carry significance in a question or statement because they direct your attention to what's important. For our purposes, we will group them into four categories:

1. **Subject area words:** Your focus is on the people, things, places, and events in time we've

been discussing since Chapter 1. In "How was your meeting?" the keyword is a thing—meeting.

2. **Verbs:** Pay attention to the action or state expressed. "How are you going to beat him?" could have multiple meanings; the key to understanding the question is knowing which definition of "beat" is in play. The verb will also give you the information on when the action takes place. "How did you beat him?" refers to a fait accompli as opposed to an action that will be taken at some later time.

3. **Modifiers:** Adjectives and adverbs can become keywords when used well. (Note: In this sentence, the adverb "well" is a keyword.) Good adjectives and adverbs can become keywords. (Note: In this sentence, the adjective "good" passes as a keyword.)

4. **Directive phrases:** These are phrases such as "of course" and "without a doubt." Phrases like this are meant to present an idea or situation as being obvious; they both reflect and infuse bias into conversation and therefore should be considered keywords. A perfect example comes from a National Public Radio story on the number of vacancies in the Department of Justice a year into the Donald Trump presidency. The reporter was listing the so-called big jobs still open at the Department of Justice: "One year in, there still no one in charge of the criminal division, the national security division, the tax division,

the environment division, and of course, the civil rights division."[1] The embedded judgment in this "report" is that the Trump presidency has an agenda to assign less importance to the civil rights division than to others. This is analogous to your client for web design services saying to you, "You are scheduling me for next month, of course, because you have much bigger clients who need immediate attention, right?"

Keywords in Questions

Your client emails you this question: "Why are we meeting at eleven o'clock a.m. on Pennsylvania Avenue when the parade starts there in the early afternoon?" A text or email with that question leaves the question open for interpretation. You can't be certain what the keywords are. However, if she calls you, she would make it clear:

"Why are we meeting at *eleven o'clock a.m.* on Pennsylvania Avenue when the parade starts there in the early afternoon?" The emphasis makes the time key to understanding, so you could respond with, "Good point. Let's have a breakfast meeting at 8:30."

"Why are we meeting at eleven o'clock a.m. on *Pennsylvania Avenue*" suggests a desire to shift the meeting location. Your response would be linked to location rather than time.

Keywords in Answers

In 2006, *MIT Technology Review* did an analysis called "What's the Best Q&A Site?" to determine which of the many question-and-answer websites had followers who tended to give the most accurate, complete responses. They were essentially looking for sites where the respondents use some of the same skills we cover in this book. The data collected gives great insights into how keywords affect the quality of an answer.

The author of the article, Wade Roush, posed the same two questions to a variety of sites:

⬦ "Why did the Mormons settle in Utah?"

⬦ "What is the best way to make a grilled cheese sandwich?"[2]

Roush's keywords focus on people (Mormons) and place (Utah) in the first question. His keywords in the second question are an adjective (best) and a thing (grilled cheese sandwich). The only way to give a quality response to those questions is to put the focus on Mormons in Utah and best grilled cheese sandwich, respectively. Easy, right? Not so much for some of the respondents.

Contrast a good response with a bad one for each. The good response honors the keywords *and* integrates more than a single subject area—people, place, thing, and time—into the answer.

"Why did the Mormons settle in Utah?"

GOOD

> The church believes that God directed Brigham Young, Joseph Smith's successor as president of the church, to call for the Mormons to organize and migrate west, beyond the Western frontier of the United States to start their own community away from traditional American society.

BAD

> Joseph Smith told them to stop there.

"What is the best way to make a grilled cheese sandwich?"

GOOD

> There is no "best" way. It's the cheese that makes the difference. I'd use sharp Colby or similar . . . My daughter puts sliced tomatoes inside . . . As for me, I like to use two slices of bread. Spread feta cheese on each, put yellow cheese on top of one, and cover with the other. Enjoy and use your imagination.

BAD

> The way Johnny Depp made them in the film Benny & Joon . . . with a hot iron on the ironing board.

As the bad responses indicated, sometimes people give a flippant response to a question to be funny, not to inform. That's fine for a party, but we have heard people do this in business meetings, thinking that their humor is charming. If you have the opportunity to use your knowledge of keywords to answer a question well, do it and be as clever as you like. But save the stupid humor for cocktail hour.

LEVERAGING KNOWLEDGE
OF BODY LANGUAGE

Nonverbal communication encompasses body movements from head to toe as well as vocal characteristics—not speech, but the way sounds are made—the way you handle personal space, and how you use things around you. It even includes the way you present yourself through dress and makeup, and where you choose to sit at a conference table.

A job interviewer can ask you an easy question such as "What is your greatest weakness?" but the raised pitch in the voice, tilt of the head, narrowed eyes, and smirk would tip you off to the fact that this is probably a trap question. If you don't deliver a great response, you might as well walk out the door and never look back. Suddenly, the person's body language has alerted you to the reality that this is an easy question that involves a tough response. Your awareness of that gives you a huge advantage in providing the best response and directing the conversation.

Reading Body Language

Your first task in reading someone else is to discover how a person speaks and acts when little or no stress is present. That is the person's *baseline*. Your first task in understanding your own body language is to have a good sense of your own baseline.

In Chapter 2, we gave you examples of good and bad questions and listed non-pertinent questions in the good group. When observing someone to get a sense of his or her baseline, use non-pertinent questions to put that person at ease. Regardless of the professional or personal situation, if you get someone talking about a topic that requires little or no thinking and puts the person into a comfort zone of conversation, you will see stress dissipate.

Listen for the tone of voice, pacing, other vocal qualities that come naturally. Observe energy level and style of movement. Turn the tables and have someone you trust give you insights about your baseline body language as well. Even when you're relaxed, do you use fillers like "um" or "ah"? Are you normally reserved or high energy?

Our colleague Gregory Hartley (*The Art of Body Talk*), a decorated former army interrogator who moved quickly into senior executive roles because of his unique interpersonal skills, has a simple way to help people remember the basic types of body movements. He calls them the "big four":

⋄ *Illustrators* punctuate your communication.

⋄ *Regulators* help control the flow of conversation.

⋄ *Barriers* help define your personal space.

⋄ *Adaptors* are self-soothing gestures.

ILLUSTRATORS

People commonly use arms and other body parts automatically to accent what they are saying. We all have a baseline style of using illustrators. When we deviate from that, we signal that there's a shift in how we feel. Whether the movement is more pronounced or less pronounced, it signals a shift in the person's emotional state.

Assume the photo on the left captures the woman's baseline approach to illustrators. She holds her arms close to her body even when her face clearly shows delight and surprise. In contrast, the photo on the right shows a deviation from her baseline: She is extremely excited. She just got the job of her dreams and throws her arms in the air in celebration.

Now flip the assumption: Typically, this woman is highly expressive, but when she feels stress, she closes up. You have to know her baseline in order to be certain which shift in energy and style expression is alerting you to a state change.

Sometimes people get in the habit of using certain illustrators, no matter how odd or offensive they might be, and so they become part of the person's baseline. It might be a move you would never or rarely make, but the important thing in reading body language is to remain objective and note what constitutes "normal" for other people.

The Washington Post focused on then-candidate Bernie Sanders's frequent use of finger-wagging in the run-up to the presidential election of 2016. It was an illustrator that became part of his routine moves:

> *It's a gesture familiar to anyone who's ever been warned, cautioned, scolded, told they are not very nice or otherwise belittled. A hand, often the dominant one, is raised. An index finger is extended skyward. The finger moves from left to right in a workmanlike arc.*[3]

The article concluded by noting the many politicians in history who have had signature moves that other people would consider quirky, but they were part of the person's repertoire of normal—or in our terms, baseline—moves.

Regulators

Regulators are movements and sounds you would use to encourage someone to keep talking or stop talking. The postures and movements associated with active listening encourage the other person to continue. On the flip side, when you clamp your lips while someone is talking, you are sending the signal that you don't want to hear any more or you don't want to hear more of the same. When you turn away slightly, it's the same kind of signal.

When you're busy, there is a huge temptation to send signals that encourage people to curtail their explanations, avoid repetition, and leave your office or your meeting when they are done saying what

they have to say. No matter what your rank within the company, you would be better off if you avoid any overuse of regulators that shut down communication.

Listening is one of the most powerful tools you have to affect human behavior.

If there is one key message we've learned about intelligence gathering from top people in the intel community, it's the fact that people tend to love the sound of their own voice—and if they think you love it too, they will pour their hearts and brains out to you. As a corollary, if they really think you care because you've paid attention to them and made them a priority for even a sliver of time, they will tell you all kinds of things.

In looking at the two photos on the previous page, ask yourself which woman wants to hear what you have to say. That's the expression of active listening versus the expression of shutting down a conversation.

BARRIERS

The photo on the next page illustrates different kinds of barriers. It's 1975 and the scene is the office of the CEO of Bergdorf Goodman—the upscale retail specialty store on Fifth Avenue in New York City. Three key players are seated with CEO Andrew Goodman and one of them will become the new CEO.

Andrew Goodman's barriers are abundant, but probably not because he needs to increase his comfort level, which is why barriers are often used. He has barriers as a display of importance and distance: a big gilded desk, a pile of papers, some kind of award, a pen set, and a cigarette. He also has a shoulder facing the men in his office.

The man to his immediate left is using his arms as barriers, as well as tightly locked legs, and his head. He's blocked everyone and everything in the room out of his sight. It probably wouldn't surprise you if we told you he'd recently been indicted on price-fixing charges.

The man to his left seems to have a need to close himself off as well. He's not looking at the boss and his fingers are locked.

And then we have a man with no barriers. A straightforward look at the boss, open body language, and relaxed legs crossed in the manner of a cosmopolitan gentleman. He is confident. He is Ira

Neimark, who succeeded Goodman as CEO of the company.

Barriers are very useful. They can help you establish personal space, give you the distance you require to feel comfortable, and set you up as the person in charge.

On the flip side, they can undermine your communication, intimidate people, and come across as downright rude. They can also make you look weak and afraid—like you have to hide behind something in order to have a conversation.

ADAPTORS

These are nervous movements that are self-soothing in nature. They might be grooming gestures, like brushing a piece of lint off your jacket even though there may be no lint there, or straightening a tie, or playing with your earrings or hair. They could be rubbing two fingers together.

What are your adaptors? Maryann posed this question to a mixed group of business professionals recently and one of the women proudly ticked off her list of adaptors. But while she was doing it, she was also doing a grooming gesture—playing with her necklace. Maryann asked her, "Is there anything else you think you do, other than what you've mentioned?"

"No," she said with assurance. She was sure she she'd nailed it.

Every person around her who'd watched her got a good laugh out of that and she had no idea what they thought was so funny.

Culture and Context

Review the following collection of hand gestures, all of which are offensive somewhere. When Maryann was presenting to a large multicultural audience at a university, she asked anyone in the audience if they had a strong negative reaction to any of the gestures and asked them to explain why. One audience member jumped up and shouted, "Never do that!" He wasn't pointing to the raised middle finger. He was pointing to what most of us know as the "okay" sign. In Greece, Spain, Brazil, and Turkey it

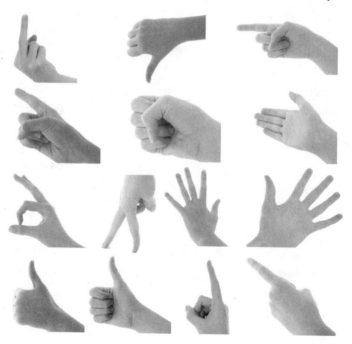

is not considered an appropriate gesture. It's either offensive, or it's sexual in nature. Another person, from an Arab nation, noted that the thumbs up was incredibly rude where he came from. Then there's the *moutza*—hand outstretched with the palm facing the other person—which is an offensive gesture to Greeks.

Training in intercultural relations has become common due to our global economy, so your awareness of these gestures may be high. Our focus is on a narrower definition of culture and how the culture—or cultures—to which we belong affects the ways we use body language. This includes the way we move, speak, and dress.

For example, if your background is in the theater, there are normal behaviors within the culture of the theater. Over-the-top illustrators may be common. One person would prefer to be the center of attention over another person and uses illustrators and regulators to make that a reality. Actually, we shouldn't limit this to theater because people in companies who want to be the center of attention will do the same kind of thing.

There are cultures associated with gangs, political parties, skydivers, alcoholics, and kids in a strict boarding school. The point is that baselining is a critical skill for you, and when baselining, it's essential that you not use your own culture as the basis for evaluating what is or is not normal for another person. When baselining, you're focused on what's normal for that person, not what is normal for you.

Another factor affecting your filters when base-lining is context. We have a tendency to project meaning based on our own experiences. That's perfectly normal, but projection gets in the way of baselining.

What is the baby orangutan doing? Well, we just don't know if he's eating, picking his teeth, sucking his finger because it hurts, or anything else. We have no context. To complicate matters, our projection is strictly human. To make a judgment about

the meaning of this image with no other information about that orangutan reflects a disregard for
data. When you are reading body language, you
may involve your valuable intuition, but data
should play a role in your conclusions.

VOCALICS

Vocalics is an area of nonverbal communication
studies because it's about how something is said
rather than what is being said. Vocal quality, emphasis, and use of fillers can indicate the presence
of stress. Being aware that stress or some level of
emotion has crept into the questioning process is
important for you if you are the one expected to respond; similarly, if you hear yourself sounding different in answering a question, you are giving away
a "secret" about how you feel.

Vocal qualities like pitch, tone, pace, volume,
and stridency can change from moment to moment, reflecting a deviation from the speaker's
baseline. Pitch often changes when a person is uncertain about information. In answering a question,
a rise in pitch is a subliminal way of communicat-
ing that. You might as well ask, "You believe me,
don't you?" Many people also have a tendency to
change the volume of their speaking when they
are uncertain of an answer. Some get louder—as
though the extra volume conveys authority—and
some get softer, hoping that you don't hear what
they are saying.

A quality such as stridency suggests stress only when it isn't normal for the person. When the vocal chords tighten up and/or the throat becomes dry, the voice takes on a different sound. It can get raspy, the way comedian Joan Rivers used to sound all the time; it was part of her baseline. Look for other signs of stress, like an increase in the blink rate. If the throat is drying out due to stress, then the eyes are drying out too.

Earlier in the chapter, we referenced the importance of emphasis in determining keywords. "Why are we meeting at *eleven o'clock a.m.* on Pennsylvania Avenue when the parade starts there in the early afternoon?" suggests something different when the emphasis is on the location, not the time.

Use of fillers is part of the baseline for some people. A lot of people use the word "like" constantly. It's annoying, ubiquitous, and meaningless. Many of us who are trained to avoid fillers may succeed in not doing ums and ahs, but we still find ourselves using a silent filler, otherwise known as a pause. The main thing to note is that, if it's not part of the person's baseline, then it may be time to probe into why there is a gap in the conversation.

PROXIMITY AND SPACE

How close or far away you are to someone can influence communication. Also, where you choose to be in a room can make a difference in your interaction.

Let's say you're interacting with a customer that you've done business with and feel comfortable with.

The person is asking you about an upgrade to a product and you find yourself wanting to keep your distance. Maybe you even leave the room briefly and when you return, you sit in a chair that's a little further from the one you were in before. That's a distinct message that you don't want to let the person in. Maybe you feel threatened by the question because you know you don't have a good answer. Your behavior is signaling a problem; even without body language training, the customer senses something is off.

The concept of territoriality is also encompassed by this field of study. So even though you may be across the room from your customer, when you sit in his favorite chair, you may get the same kind of response as if you leaned forward and invaded his personal space.

Where you choose to sit can also make a difference in your communication. Maryann once saw a candidate for a midlevel management position stride into the conference room where the interview was being held and sit at the head of the table. The president of the company thought that should be his seat; the interview went downhill from there.

Using Body Language

The fundamental advice we can give you is to stay consistent with your natural style. If you want to see some hilarious examples of how not to use body language—what impression it makes when people go against their natural styles—do an online search for "funny body language videos." One that comes up is Sheldon Cooper of the *Big Bang Theory* learning how to counter his robotic presentation style.[4]

OPEN VERSUS CLOSED

The basic differences in body language styles are open and closed. Open body language is invitational; it suggests you want to share ideas, share your space, and display trust in the other person. Closed body language conveys the opposite impression. The difference is obvious in these photos. Even though the man on the right has a smile on his face, he is guarded, putting his portfolio between him and the other person as well as crossing his legs to suggest another physical barrier.

Some people learn to use open illustrators when they are coached in public speaking. For example, they might be told that extending a hand with the palm upward is invitational, so they insert the action into the presentation. That can work well, but make sure the way you use the illustrator is consistent with your natural style.

ENERGY LEVELS

You can choose to modify your energy level as a way to build rapport, take charge, shorten a meeting, and so on. When you do that, you impact the way other people perceive you. They might perceive you as more or less threatening, more or less competent, more or less committed to whatever you're doing. Ask yourself what outcome you want with the other person or persons. If you want the individual to talk openly to you, to come clean about something, then your energy needs to be in sync with the other person's. You may be very passionate about whatever subject is on the table, for example, but if your energy is way above the other person's, then your passion is potentially getting in the way of two-way communication.

MINIMIZING PROJECTION

Just as we might want to jump to a conclusion about what the baby orangutan in the photo was doing, people around us are projecting what our actions mean and what mood we're in. In any projection, filters play a disproportionately large role in analysis, which turns analysis into interpretation.

The reason why you want to dress and act appropriately for whatever setting you are in and whatever people you are with is to keep the focus on what you have to say. The more you seem out of place, the more the other person is likely to try to interpret what you are saying and doing rather than objectively listening and observing.

BUYING TIME

Certain actions can buy you time as you think about answering a question. The tilt of a head, a slight finger wag, a knit brow—all of these might get you a few extra seconds to craft a response that's clearer and more comprehensive than a spontaneous one.

EXERCISES

Keyword

Use keywords to help you remember jokes. It's a useful, life-of-the-party exercise to focus on the elements of a sentence or question that matter most.

Read the following joke *once,* and then see if your attention to keywords helps you retell it a few minutes later.

> *A man is walking in a graveyard when he hears the Third Symphony played backward. When it's over, the Second Symphony starts playing, also backward, and then the First. "What's going on?" he asks a cemetery worker.*

"It's Beethoven," says the worker. "He's decomposing."

(You don't have to think it's funny; you just have to remember it.)

Body Language

Disney and Pixar made the wonderful movie called *Inside Out*, with images such as the following freely available. This brilliant piece of animation is about an eleven-year-old girl's emotions. In color, you can see that anger is red, sadness is blue, and so on, but even without the color, the body language of each emotion character makes it clear what he or she represents. Your exercise is to watch a portion of any animated movie with the sound off and identify the emotions being expressed.

PART II

APPLYING THE
SKILL SET

CHAPTER 6
. . . .
JOB INTERVIEWS

"What do they want to know?"

"What are they going to ask?"

These two questions haunt job candidates from the moment they get the email to show up for an interview to the moment they walk through the company's front door. They shake hands, say "no thank you" to coffee, and sit up straight in a chair. Instead of preparing to answer predictable questions about themselves, they are still falling victim to the earworm that those two questions have become.

We suggest a shift in the mental preparation. There will be questions in the interview focused on your competence and character, but think of the interview itself as a conversation. If you have a strategy to encourage interaction—and we are giving you that here—then your responses to questions open the door to conversation.

A STRATEGY TO ENCOURAGE INTERACTION

Your strategy to turn a standard question-and-answer interview into a conversation requires three actions:

1. Identifying the type of question that you are being asked.

2. Weaving more than one subject area into the answer.

3. Active listening.

You will have a much easier time accomplishing all three if you aren't a nervous wreck, so the first tips we're going to offer involve taking your emotions down so your mental abilities rise up.

Tactics to Take Tension Down

Many people enter a mild state of fight, flight, or freeze when walking into a job interview. Unfortunately, the physiological responses to this state undermine your ability to make a great impression. Among the changes that occur are blood flowing away from your brain and into your muscles so that you are prepared to act, and your chest pounds—an annoying reminder that you are stressed out.

Before you go into the interview, find a private spot like the bathroom. Take a deep breath and throw your arms in the air with tremendous power. Straighten up so you feel as strong and in control as possible. Smile. Hold that power posture. Rest a few seconds and do it again until you feel like your head is clear and your personal power is flowing through your body. Then go to the interview.

Steps that help you counter the nervous feeling once you're in the interview include these:

◇ Deliberately slow your breathing.

◇ Try to do something physical. If it helps to move around a bit, you might walk to the table where there's a pitcher of water and pour yourself a glass.

◇ If you're sitting down, order your muscles to relax. Drop your shoulders, sit up straight so your neck is stretched out. Open your hands. Put your feet flat on the floor.

◇ You need to put your brain into an analytical mode. Focus on the other person's body language. Is he tense too? Is he doing anything, deliberately or inadvertently, that's triggering a stress response in you? Is the person using verbal cues that are setting you off? Is it the power this person has in your life right now that's making you stress out? The important action here is to think, not feel.

Beginning with the power move can trigger a significant state change; you replace the perception of weakness with the feeling of strength. The other actions you can take during the interview will support you in trying to keep that feeling coursing through your body.

Identifying Question Types

We did an exercise as part of our preparation for this book that we recommend to you. It will be particularly useful if you are preparing for a job interview, a media interview, or another encounter with a major question-and-answer component.

Throughout the day, when someone asks you a question, categorize it. The question will pertain to a particular subject, that is, person, place, thing, or event in time.

At first glance, that seems easy. Consider how context, intent of the questioner, and your own agenda and priorities can affect what type of question it is, though. To start exploring how the type of question may not be as obvious as you might think, think through ten of the most common questions in an interview:

⬦ What is your greatest strength?

⬦ What is your greatest weakness?

⬦ What do you want me to know about you?

⬦ How would your last boss and coworkers describe you?

⬦ Why should we hire you?

⬦ Why are you leaving your current job? (Or why did you leave your last job?)

◇ Why do you want this job?

◇ What was your single greatest accomplishment in your last job?

◇ What has been your greatest professional challenge?

◇ What is your ultimate career goal?

How would you classify each of them—people, thing, place, or time? The answer is not necessarily straightforward because it may depend on your goals in wanting the job. It could also depend on the job itself. For example, "Why should we hire you?" could be any type of question:

◇ **People:** You want a job in human resources. Daily, you would need to field concerns and requests from employees with problems and needs. A core job requirement is good interpersonal skills.

◇ **Thing:** You know the company needs software engineers with your unique expertise; it's the thing that should make you more desirable than anyone else.

◇ **Place:** The job is in Southeast Asia, and while lots of Americans might be able to do it, they don't want to move to Southeast Asia.

◇ **Time:** You have immediate availability, and the company has an immediate need.

The answer to "Why are you leaving your current job?" could be equally multifaceted. First and foremost, be authentic.

⬦ **People:** You are drawn to the ethos and human energy of the hiring company.

⬦ **Thing:** You've maxed out on what you can do there and see a chance to contribute at the hiring company.

⬦ **Place:** Your energy gets sapped by a ninety-minute commute every day.

⬦ **Time:** Layoffs are imminent at my company; the time to move is now.

Weaving In More than One Subject

Once you feel comfortable quickly identifying the type of question, it's time to make a conscious effort to add the other three elements to your answer. If you don't want to do that at the time, then just remember the question and think about what you could have said.

For example, a typical job interview question is, "What is your greatest strength?" This is essentially a "thing" question. A typical answer for a management position might be, "I invest a lot in planning." That is potentially a good answer, but only 25 percent of a great answer.

Here's a way to weave in all the subject areas:

A great general once said, "Plans are nothing; planning is everything," and I invest a lot of in

planning with my team. Then, whether we're to-
gether in the office or on a call, we share a sense
of purpose, timing, and methods.

Bringing in more than one subject area at a time
is skill that demands practice. You may find at
first that you have no trouble weaving in people,
but seem to have a mental block when it comes to
time—or vice versa. Being adept in covering one
type of information over another is normal. Getting
past the block with preparation will not only make
you a better interviewee but also a better storyteller.

Another way to do the same exercise is to listen
to news or talk shows and consider alternative ways
of answering the questions the interviewee was
asked. Fox News anchor Chris Wallace sat down for
a friendly interview with former NFL guard Der-
rick Dockery, who left football after ten years to join
House of Representatives Speaker Paul Ryan's staff.
Wallace began by asking him: "Which is tougher:
politics or football?"

I was born to play football. And now having to
transition from the field to the hill obviously was
a tough transition, but with the help of a great
team around me, it's easy now.[1]

In a straightforward way, Dockery brought place
(field to hill), people (team), and time (now) into the
answer to a "thing" question.

Here is how Jim answered a question posed by
Maryann, as well as the subsequent analysis. The

hypothetical job is training staff technicians who maintain electronic equipment the company sells to clients.

"HOW DID YOU GET ALONG WITH YOUR MOST RECENT BOSS?"

My most recent boss came on board just last year, and it was a process of getting into a rhythm with him. He listened to how we do our jobs, and then he wanted us to demonstrate our capabilities. He wanted to know what we do in the office and onsite with customers.

I appreciated that he wanted to know about the quality of interaction with our client. I gave him specific examples of what I did, quantified the results in terms of follow-on contracts, and invited him to join me on client calls. That solidified our working relationship.

Analysis:

◇ This is a "thing" question; the interviewer wants to know something like "good," "not so good," or "okay."

◇ The answer includes all subject areas:

» how long there had been interaction with the most recent boss.

» the fact that the job was done in multiple locations.

» insight into the boss, who cared about the quality of contacts with clients.

◇ The answer also adds critical, relevant "thing" information such as:

  » Your action resulted in follow-on contracts.

  » You felt confident enough to invite him on client calls with you.

◇ The initial part of the answer both baits the interviewer and helps frame the answer. It baits in the sense that it doesn't answer the question, although it strongly suggests that a positive answer is imminent. The interviewer expects to hear how the candidate got into a rhythm with the boss.

◇ The answer is fewer than 100 words, so despite the detail, this requires only twenty-five seconds to deliver.

  » The answer can be bifurcated into a "we" and an "I" response as the paragraphing suggests. The value of this is that "we" answers share credit and perspective, but "I" answers mean, "I did it!" An "I" response claims full responsibility for the action—and that means you claim full credit for it.

The alternative answer is, "Just great!" That tells the interviewer absolutely nothing of value. You've wasted a few seconds being direct, when you could have spent a few more seconds being complete.

Many websites list popular job interview questions and suggest the best ways to answer them. Our answers don't necessarily conflict with those you will find on the top websites, however, our focus on weaving in all the subject areas is different and gives you more advantages for these reasons:

◇ You first identify what kind of question it is: people, thing, place, or time.

◇ You have a framework for every response. If you've identified the question as a "thing" question, your brain immediately focuses on how people, place, and time information help strengthen the answer. (If one of the subject areas doesn't work for your answer, just drop it from the framework.)

◇ You give color and distinction to the answer. Weaving in more than one subject area often means giving an example or telling a short story to make your point. Instead of sounding like the audio version of your resume, you bring the resume to life.

Going through four of the previous sample questions, let's look generically at how some or all four subject areas could be used in responses to them to deliver the most compelling narrative about yourself as a job candidate.

"WHAT IS YOUR GREATEST STRENGTH?"

This comes across as primarily a "thing" question because the expected response is a skill or skill set required for the job. What we have seen as recommended answers logically tend to focus on that. Our logic is a little different, though.

Step back from the expected response and figure out what you would say if the question came from a friend. Among the answers might be your sense of hospitality (people), facility doing mental math (thing), adaptability in different environments (place), and ability to process information quickly (time).

How does your genuine, greatest strength apply to the job you want? You are in a position to respond with clarity and authenticity if you give the answer to that question. The alternative is inserting vocabulary from the job description into an answer. It's a robotic answer like, "I have excellent verbal and written communication and presentation skills."

An alternative might be:

> *Storytelling. Whether I'm writing or talking with people, anchoring a message with a good story is my strong suit. I make it relevant and keep it short.*

With a response like that, you don't waste ten words, you deliver twenty-seven good ones that cover the areas of thing, people, and time to start a conversation. Needless to say, regardless of whether you give the "job description" answer or the engaging one, you must be prepared to follow it up with specific examples.

"WHAT IS YOUR GREATEST WEAKNESS?"

In providing a reference for a job candidate, Maryann was asked by a recruiter, "What is her greatest weakness?" Maryann responded by telling her one of her greatest strengths: "Diligence."

"Excuse me?" the woman asked.

"Diligence and reliability are weaknesses when you put the needs of the company and the team above your own needs. In other words, she has a tendency to push herself hard—sometimes too hard—in order to get the job done right."

The woman got the job. The point is that being asked about a weakness is an opportunity to talk about a strength.

If you know the reason you have been late for a few meetings and late in delivering a few reports in your last job is that you have children who do unpredictable things, then occasional lateness may be your greatest weakness from a corporate perspective. That is not inherently a negative, however:

> My greatest weakness is my children. My husband and I are meticulous in scheduling, but sometimes even the best-laid plans run off the track.

The elements of time, context, and people support the explanation of your "greatest weakness," that is, delays due to your children's needs. But you didn't present your weakness as lateness: You presented it as family. This response would not work with every interviewer, of course; this is a case when doing your homework about the interviewer could make the difference! (Note: Always do an online search on the interviewer before you go to the meeting.)

Another example of a common weakness is a basic administrative requirement—paperwork. In that case, your weakness might be expressed as "competitiveness." You focus on closing the deal to the detriment of your "household chores." Admitting that shortcoming is an entrée to talking about your accomplishments.

"WHAT WAS YOUR SINGLE GREATEST ACCOMPLISHMENT IN YOUR LAST JOB?"

When Maryann posed the following question to Jim, he had no idea what the question would be in our exercise, and therefore, had no time to prepare. It was one way of checking out if we could do what we were asking you to do!

"What was your single greatest accomplishment in your last job?"

> I was able to fulfill a lifelong dream that began when I was ten years old—to invent something. The president gave me the opportunity, the funding, and the mission to save the company money and enhance the training ability of our company by inventing a device called the electronic language simulator.

Jim's answer wove in all four subject areas, with the "time" part of the response humanizing the answer in a memorable way.

When asked about your greatest accomplishment in a job interview, don't be hemmed in by the description of the job you are applying for. Just as Jim opened with an authentic statement about a life-long dream, give the response that's true for you. If you feel your greatest accomplishment was getting your company to sponsor *Science Friday* (Public Radio International), you should say that. It provides insight into you and fodder for conversation; that is, the response is multidimensional and stimulates interaction rather than leading to a dead-end like, "Uh huh. Okay. Wow. Thanks."

"WHY DO YOU WANT THIS JOB?"

A number of years ago, Jim interviewed people for full- and part-time sales positions at the famous Forest Lawn Memorial Park, now the permanent home of celebrities such as Michael Jackson and Elizabeth Taylor. He found that people who really wanted the job but didn't need it were generally unsuccessful. People who desperately needed the job also tended to be unsuccessful. People who presented a balance of want and need had the highest rate of success. No doubt, Jim is not the only hiring manager who found that to be true with potential salespeople.

The challenge is integrating "need" without sounding needy. The way to do that is to weave in all four subjects. In the summer of 2015, *TheStreet* ran an article entitled "10 Tech Companies with the Highest Paying Sales Jobs." Combining base pay plus commission, the total annual pay for these jobs ranged from $150,000 to $191,000.[2]

If you were a candidate for one of these jobs, it's easy to see why you would want it. But how could you express your need? Here is one possibility:

> *I both want and need this job because it's part of my career plan. Ten years ago, I designed the trajectory of my sales career. I cultivated interpersonal skills as I built up my knowledge of this industry. Based on how I see my career taking shape, this job is a dream come true.*

Active Listening

Active listening is one of the most critical tools you can have in building rapport with someone. It's a magical way of getting people to connect with you and share information.

Active listening has three components: physical, intellectual, and emotional.

The intellectual component involves listening for keywords, which might be indicated by emphasis or how frequently they are used. For example, you have no military background, but the person interviewing you is a Navy officer. He talks about ships, not boats. So, you talk about ships, not boats. Adopting keywords shows you are paying attention.

Sometimes keywords give an overt message. If the person interviewing you makes a few references to taking a break or getting away for a while, she might actually be focused on her upcoming vacation. Maybe that has more of her attention than your job interview. In a case like that, the person may be either extra chatty or rushing to get the job done. Active listening will help you move the pace of the conversation accordingly.

Your body language—including your tone, pitch, and pace of speaking—can signal to the other person

that you are listening carefully. Keep your focus on the person you're talking with, but avoid staring. Use mirroring to promote a sense of relationship between you. Mirroring does not mean mimicking; it is positioning your body comfortably in a way similar to the other person. People do this naturally when they feel a connection to another person.

The emotional part of active listening is realizing that you are in a conversation, even though it's called a "job interview." Be normal: If the person interviewing you shows some emotion, there is a quid pro quo in play. In other words, it's the exchange of "something for something," or "this for that." Express enough emotion to show that you care and want to connect with the person, but keep your personal life to yourself. This is about listening and exhibiting empathy, not about exposing your deep dark secrets or greatest longings.

EXERCISES

If you are currently going through job interviews, then we recommend you do this exercise with each of the ten popular interview questions. On the other hand, if you are lubricating your brain cells for a future experience in interviewing, then we recommend focusing on these two questions and answering them with the four subject areas in mind:

⬦ What has been your greatest professional
challenge?

⬦ What is your ultimate career goal?

Tips

These questions involve superlatives—"greatest"
and "ultimate"—so the answer to both is something
significant. Your greatest professional challenge
would not be moving your office from one floor to
another.

Each could focus primarily on a person, place,
thing, or event in time. You want to be honest, but
you also want to consider the nature of the position
you're applying for. If you want a job in sales, leading with a "thing" as your greatest challenge might
not be so bad ("Our signature product needed up-
dating"). One the other hand, leading with "people" could get you in trouble ("Our sales team had
some real slackers on it").

When someone asks you about a superlative
like your best or worst moment, the highest point
in your last job, and so on, let your body language
rise to the occasion. You don't want an over-the-
top display of emotion, however, using your hands
and face to express your point is appropriate when
talking about an unparalleled experience.

CHAPTER 7
. . . .
NEGOTIATIONS AND SALES

Golden Balls is a British game show featuring negotiation in the final round. It's a derivation of a strategy game called Prisoner's Dilemma, designed to demonstrate how two supposedly rational people might not cooperate with each other even though it appears to be in their best interests to cooperate.

In *Golden Balls*, having accumulated a certain pot of money, two contestants must choose either a golden ball with the word "split" inside, or one with the word "steal." If both contestants choose "split," they split the winnings earned. If both choose "steal," they both go home with nothing. If one chooses "split" and one chooses "steal," the person choosing "steal" gets all the money.

The two contestants negotiate to arrive at what each sees as the best deal. The techniques they use can be distilled down to silence/compliance, guarantee, and bait and switch. Each involves body language cues as well as verbal ones. If the contestants were trained in body language, they would likely tip each other off. If they were trained in the kind of response cues we explore in this book, they would also tip each other off.

Maryann was once in a negotiation with a high-powered executive in which she used silence to get what she wanted. She had just coached him and a few of his colleagues in reading and using body language to detect deception. She wanted to turn this into a consulting gig, so when he asked, "Would you be able to come back and help our human resources department in screening applicants for certain jobs?" she wanted to shout, "Yes!" Instead, she smiled slightly. Not getting a verbal response, he filled the dead air by explaining to her why she should help them—essentially negotiating her part of the deal for her.

Sometimes the best response to a question is not answering it with words.

The three techniques mentioned earlier have shown up in the final round of *Golden Balls* in some interesting ways, and the lessons are applicable in all kinds of negotiations and sales situations. Before exploring them, however, look at how people handle Prisoner's Dilemma—and how knowing that helps you strategically in business interactions.

THE PRISONER'S DILEMMA

The excellent, and now ended, television show called *The Closer* used the Prisoner's Dilemma several times to extract a confession from a murderer. *The Closer* features an interrogator (Jim's background) who commands all the interpersonal management skills that interrogators use in a negotiation with a prisoner—in selling him the idea that cooperation yields the optimal outcome.

The premise of the Prisoner's Dilemma is that two people are caught committing a crime and may or may not have committed a worse crime. The two are separated and police try to press them into giving incriminating information. Their options are:

⬦ Admit the other person committed the worse crime, and you won't be held for the minor one. You do zero time, but the other person will get a five-year sentence.

⬦ If you don't rat on him, and he rats on you, then you are the one who gets a five-year sentence and he goes free.

⬦ You and your fellow prisoner know the evidence against you is merely circumstantial. If you stick together and accept the sentence for the minor crime, never trying to incriminate each other for the worse crime, you both go to jail for only a year.

◇ If you both betray each other, you both face a penalty for the worse crime.

In *Golden Ball* terms, it's

◇ Split-steal

◇ Steal-split

◇ Split-split

◇ Steal-steal

Running the numbers on the prison sentences given as examples, the most predictable, positive outcome for both people involves cooperating. Each gets a one-year term. But as soon as one person thinks that the other will stay silent (the "split" ball), then she is better off incriminating the other. There is also the possibility each will point the finger at the other person—hoping that the other person stays silent. This has nothing to do with truth, of course, and everything to do with strategy.

A critical piece of this strategic thinking is that a "prisoner's" best option is cooperating *only if* that person has no control over what the other person does. What we are telling you is that you *can* control what the other person does in some real-life examples of Prisoner's Dilemma. Later in the chapter, Scenario #2 illustrates how this is done both in the game show and in a sales negotiation.

Prisoner's Dilemma forces people to decide if the good of the group supersedes the benefits to the individual. But why would a rational person cooperate when his own ass is on the line? Answer: He wouldn't—unless the benefits of cooperation exceed the benefits of going in for the kill.

In a business situation, probably one of the most dramatic examples of this is the deal that the oil company BP made with the United States Department of Justice over the *Deepwater Horizon* tragedy. Eleven people were killed and 1,300 miles of coastline were fouled after BP's offshore rig blew up on April 20, 2010, and oil spilled for eighty-seven days into the Gulf of Mexico from the Macondo well. But BP and DOJ chose "split," allowing each to take home assets of comparable value. DOJ could claim financial assets from a multi-billion-dollar settlement and political assets from extracting a record-setting payout from a company. BP could claim the privilege of future oil and gas leases in the Gulf of Mexico and other US-controlled areas as well as a "get out of jail free" pass for its senior executives. Split-split.

A very high-profile, high-stakes "game" of Prisoner's Dilemma has determined how between 50 percent and 70+ percent of stocks are traded in the United States. These trades are not executed on the basis of a human decision, but rather by an algorithm "at a speed, rate, and scale that is beyond our comprehension,"[1] according to author Andrew Zolli (*Resilience: Why Things Bounce Back*). In a matter of seconds—or less—someone or something stands to make millions of dollars.

Jad Abumrad, the host of the radio show focusing on this phenomenon, discovered that in the late 20th century, it took eleven or twelve seconds to execute a trade because humans controlled the process. Because a basic law of the stock market is "the fastest person will usually win,"[2] traders became more and more dependent on the transmission speed of information. These were speeds they could not process, so computers and algorithms became the primary tools to execute trades. The high-stakes Prisoner's Dilemma starts to take shape at this point.

Physical proximity of computers to the trading floor held huge significance. The closer your computer was to the computers with information on the stocks, the faster you got the data you needed to make a smart trade. Then the people controlling the real estate and access to the exchange upped the ante: Pay us enough and you can come inside.

Everyone wants to "steal."

In 2006, "inside" became 20,000 square feet of space to accommodate the computers of traders. The "decisions" of these computers are transmitted to an adjacent room to decide on buying or selling. And note well: the cabling on each of these computers is precisely the same length as the next one to avoid providing any transmission-speed advantage to one computer resident over another.

Everyone is forced to "split."

Abumrad continued: "You would think that since all machines can now be inside the exchange— literally inside the market building—that the speed race would be over. Right? No. It only gets worse."[3]

With thirteen regulated exchanges as well as nonpublic markets—totaling more than sixty—there are speed races among all of them. Transactions are now, in 2018, measured in roughly eight-millisecond increments, and that is likely to change before you turn the page of this book. Abumrad asks, "Are we fast enough now? Can we stop?" and Manoj Narang, who was CEO of the high-frequency trading company Tradeworx at the time, answered:

> *We would love to stop this arms race. The arms race is a huge drain on resources. . .*

> *We're not going to call a truce because there's such thing in game theory called Prisoner's Dilemma.*[4]

Moving the discussion to a more common business challenge, this is the head-to-head interaction that two local restaurants might have about advertising. They are the two primary, high-end restaurants in a small resort community. What they offer is essentially identical. The executive chefs of both restaurants have graduated from the Culinary Institute of America and earned good reputations. Their cuisine, prices, and presentation are comparable on every level.

Decision: Agree not to advertise at all, agree to advertise, or don't agree on either and see what happens. With the Prisoner's Dilemma criteria in mind, here is how this might work out:

◇ The two restaurants agree not to advertise at all. Purely by chance, about half the target population, both local and visiting, will come to each restaurant.

  » Each week, each restaurant makes $5,000.

◇ The two restaurants agree to advertise. Once again, they both earn the same amount, but each also spends $1,000/week on advertising.

  » Each comes away with $4,000.

◇ The restaurants do not agree. One advertises and gets 80 percent of the market share.

  » Weekly earnings go to $8,000, but $1,000 was spent on advertising, so the weekly take is $7,000.

◇ The non-advertiser spends no money on ads and gets 20 percent of the market share.

  » The non-advertiser makes only $2,000.

The ideal situation for both is to not advertise, but both restaurants see that advertising will always make them more money. They have an incentive to talk to each other and agree on what to do, but they have no obligation to each other. Unlike the prisoners, they have the advantage of building a relationship with each other to get the best outcome.

That is precisely what the contestants in *Golden Balls* are invited to do. Yet we see time and again that two people or two companies will not choose to cooperate if they have a shot at winning the big prize.

What's going on is a paradox. People are often willing to hurt themselves when they are selfishly focused on their own well-being.

Whatever industry you are in, consider under what circumstances you or your senior executives are asked to "split" or "steal."

GOLDEN BALLS GO TO WORK

Three scenarios are described in the following section, and each one uses different combinations of the techniques previously listed to create the best outcome. To begin, we want to define the techniques as we use them in in this context:

⬦ "Silence / compliance" means the person is reserved, speaking very little or not at all, and there is a hint of agreement with the other individual.

⬦ "Guarantee" means the person assertively expresses a position and backs it up with promise.

⬦ "Bait and switch" means the person changes direction after strongly suggesting one course of action. (This is not to be confused with bait-and-switch advertising, which involves luring customers in with a lower price and then trying to get them to buy a higher priced item.)

After the scenarios, we offer examples of how they apply to workplace interactions—and how you can use body language and verbal cues to establish an advantage. As you read through them, think of examples of your own—either those you've experienced, or some that could occur in your workplace.

Scenario #1

THE GAME

A man and woman have accumulated winnings of £100,150 (roughly $150,000). Both display emotion with their body language when told how large the prize is. The man immediately remarks that this is an easy decision; he looks both confident and resigned: he will choose to "split," and the audience knows that even before he shows the ball he has chosen.

The man telegraphs precisely what he intends to do, putting the woman in the superior position to determine the outcome. In contrast to her competitor, the woman remains silent in the beginning, eventually saying something that goads him into giving a heartfelt commitment to splitting the money. Then, sweetly, she says, "Everyone who knew me would be disgusted if I stole the money." She keeps her gaze on the man and says, "Please." He keeps prattling, swearing that he will split the money.

She utters the word, "Promise." Without hesitation, he says, "I am going to split."

At that point, the woman purses her lips—an action that often suggests the person is holding something back. She takes her gaze off her competitor and puts it on the host. You now have enough training in body language to see that a face like the one in the picture is telling you not to trust what comes out of her mouth!

When told to pick up the ball each chooses, she looks at the host while the man grabs his "split" ball. Then she flashes "steal."

His technique is "guarantee." Hers begins with "silence/compliance" and morphs into "bait and switch."

The woman's win is not enough to counter her feelings of betrayal. Her lips purse again. She relaxes them for a second, and then purses them once again as she turns her glance to the host, abandoning the distraught competitor. She then turns completely away from the table, showing her back to both the host and her competitor. As if that were not enough to suggest how she feels, she covers her mouth with her hand.

The woman admits in a later interview that she did it out of revenge because of something the man had done to her earlier in the show. She felt highly motivated to go against her nature, but her motivation was not greed.

THE APPLICATION

If something like this happened in the workplace, the "winner" might feel so guilt ridden that she would express remorse and perhaps show more transparency and kindness in future dealings with coworkers. In a game show, the win is the end of the story.

A workplace version of this is not uncommon if you consider the interaction in a generic way. The situation might be a small team dedicated to a creative effort, like a marketing campaign. Everyone agrees it's a "we" effort; the negotiation is complete among members of the team. Then the client gets a sneak peek at what's happening and seems thrilled.

Suddenly, an ambitious member of the team leaks signs that she wants to make it an "I" effort; she plans to use her "steal" ball.

To gain control over the conversation before that happens, first you need to spot the body language and verbal cues that your teammate is about to "steal." They may include:

◇ Evasive actions, such as those the female contestant used—eyes moving away from the team and focused on the client, lips pressed together, and moving away from the rest of the team by pushing a chair back or taking a few steps away.

◇ A shift from "we" to "I" in conversation.

◇ Emphasizing aspects of the presentation that legitimately are more "I" than "we."

After you've identified the signs, then act:

◇ Ask the client a question that rivets attention to you and/or the rest of the team. For example, if the teammate trying to "steal" had the lead on visual elements of the presentation, have your question draw attention to the text.

◇ Listen for keywords in the response that allow you to continue to focus on team effort. For example, if the client has some confusion about the text, then ask good narrative questions to keep the focus on it:

» How could it be better?

» What message do you want it to convey?

» Why does it fall short for you?

» Where does it succeed?

◇ Keep your body language inviting.

» Use "we," whether you are sharing credit for a job well done or blame for falling short.

» Maintain eye contact with the client.

» Make sure you are not fidgeting or using any barriers. Stay open and calm.

» Point to something, such as a whiteboard or slide, where you can establish a common point of focus with the client.

In the situation of a teammate going rogue, identifying that the value of your work is about to be diminished is the first step to enforcing "split" and countering "steal." It puts you on the road to controlling the conversation.

Scenario #2

THE GAME

From the beginning of this negotiation, one of the contestants is smirking. His lips are sealed, and he exudes self-satisfaction. He might as well be carrying a sign that broadcasts, "I have a plan!" The other man comes across as more reserved at first, but then starts to exhibit stress. He swivels his chair and stares at the balls in front of him. He pulls at his earlobe.

The man with plan arches his eyebrow and tells his competitor to trust him: He is going to pick the "steal" ball.

The other man cannot believe what he has just heard: "Sorry?!"

Next, the smirking competitor, whose name is Nick, gives instructions to the man on the other side of the table: "I want you to split, and I promise you I will split the money with you."

The other man is incredulous. He repeats what he understands to be the deal. After the show, they will square up with Nick voluntarily giving half the money to him. He offers the logical alternative of both picking split, but Nick is adamant. No split; he will steal.

The ploy is pure genius—and here is why it worked.

By saying he will steal, Nick establishes dominance. If he sticks to his word, the other man would not want to play his "steal" ball because both would lose. If he chooses "split," however, there is chance that he will walk way (after the show) with half the money. And if he chooses to split and Nick does a turnaround, he gets half the money at the end of the show. He is boxed in.

When he realizes he is in a potentially no-win situation, the second man becomes emotional in giving Nick his guarantee that he will split. Keep in mind that emotions can undercut a person's ability to use all his cognitive powers. He is eroding his own ability to negotiate. Nick has strengthened his position even more.

After shocking his opponent by also choosing "split," Nick rubs his hands together gleefully. His bait-and-switch plan worked. Why wouldn't it? This is someone who knows the secret of the Prisoner's Dilemma.

THE APPLICATION

The backstory on this situation is useful because it spotlights the importance of preparation in negotiation. Nick is the man who won, and he has been on multiple game shows in the UK. He funds a charity with the money he has earned on television. Coming into the game with a strategy and knowing how to size up his competitor to confirm that the strategy would work, he knew he would walk away from the table with half the winnings.

As a former military interrogator and interrogation instructor, Jim knows the mechanics of the Prisoner's Dilemma better than most people. He has years of preparation every time he negotiates something. Like Nick, Jim used surprise to gain the superior position with a car salesman and ultimately created a win-win situation—on his own terms.

Jim knew he wanted to buy a more practical, family-friendly vehicle than the sports car he had sitting in his garage. He walked into a dealership and went straight to a salesman.

"How can I help you?" the man asked.

Jim's response set the negotiation in motion, although the salesman didn't realize it: "I am going to make a deal with you."

A person in that sales position expects, "I might make a deal," or "I'm just looking right now." He does not expect to be told that the customer intends to make a deal, however.

The salesman did not take Jim seriously. He threw out a number of $12,500 on the trade-in value for the sports car, but he didn't write anything down. Jim thanked him and told him he would be back to close a deal in a couple of weeks.

Two weeks later, Jim returned to the dealership and found his man. "I'm going to make a deal today," he said. The man remembered him, but he didn't remember exactly what they had talked about.

Jim said, "Well, we're starting with $15,000 for the trade-in . . ."

The man had no idea if he'd actually offered a number that high as the "ums" and "ahs" out of his mouth indicated. He was feeling a bit stressed out and boxed in—just like Nick's competitor in *Golden Balls*.

Jim closed the deal, and yes, it was to his advantage—although the salesman got a good commission on a big family car.

Jim read his mark. He saw nervous gestures, just as Nick might have noticed his opponent's pulling on his earlobe. Even without words or tone of voice, signs like this indicate that the person is feeling some emotion—and as we've said before, emotion weakens your cognitive ability. While the other person is vulnerable, it's time to close the deal.

Scenario #3

THE GAME

You may wonder how a more relevant example could be discussed than Scenario #2, in which one contestant clearly controls the outcome. In Scenario #3, we see the game played out with minor stakes and ostensibly no one caring about the result. The fact is, someone almost always cares about the stakes, no matter how small. In this case, perhaps the true nature of both competitors surfaced, and we can learn from that.

The host announced that this was one of the unluckiest rounds of *Golden Balls* in his experience. The competitors were vying for a mere £2.85, or about $4. The studio audience went crazy; these people know that it's about human behavior and not money.

The man chose "split" and the woman chose "steal," to which the host responded, "You did that out of devilment." She agreed. She admitted that she

was always going to steal; he admitted he was always going to split. Like the woman in the photo, the competitor's face showed she had a plan and would stick to it. She showed no signs of caring about the consequences, in contrast to the man, who had a playful kindness in his expression.

THE APPLICATION

To see how Scenario #3 applies in the workplace, we need an answer to the question: "Would they have approached a bigger prize the same way?" There is no way of knowing for sure, however, their behavior suggests certain tendencies.

Speculate that woman in this scenario has an innate psychological need to win, whereas the man is conflict averse and has an innate need to get along with people. The woman has a higher tolerance for risk than the man; she is more apt to leave her comfort zone than he is.

Unlike the woman in Scenario #1 who chose "steal" out of revenge, this woman might well have gone with it regardless of the stakes. Getting away with a risky strategy gratifies her. She would be the person on your sales team who doesn't mind "fear selling," a technique Jim McCormick describes in *Body Language Sales Secrets*. That is, if she senses the prospect is vulnerable, she leverages that vulnerability to win the sale.

Exercises

Part A

Use the three techniques to shape your response to a question.

Your biggest client says he wants to end the contract with your company. He asks, "What more can you do for me?"

Experiment with three different types of responses: using a guarantee, leveraging silence/compliance, and doing a bait and switch. For example, your silence/compliance tactic might be to start with, "Nothing this month," followed by a pause and then, "What about next month?"

Part B

Identify the spoken and unspoken language of the three techniques.

Watch a few commercials or a show of any kind—game show, sitcom, drama, news program—and pay attention to the techniques people use to convince each other of something.

Tips

"Guarantee" is more forceful when it is an "I" statement rather than a "we" statement. This is why the CEO of a company might do a commercial in which he takes personal responsibility for the product or service. A classic example comes from Frank

Purdue—"a tough guy who knows how to make a tender chicken"—who appeared in more than 200 commercials beginning in the 1970s.[5] Purdue put his integrity on the line in each ad by highlighting his cozy relationship with his chickens:

> *My graders reject 30 percent of the chickens the government accepts as Grade A. That's why it pays to insist on a chicken with my name on it. If you're not completely satisfied, write me and I'll give you your money back.[6]*

The body language of "guarantee" could be very open and inviting or firm and deliberate.

Open body language invites you into the person's space. There is a sense of shared vulnerability.

Firm and deliberate body language, which might involve planting a fist on a table for emphasis and/or vigorous head nodding, conveys certainty and resolution.

"Silence/compliance" gives the other person the floor. An article in *Psychology Today* suggests,

> *Silence is like a shell game. Whatever you do, you'll reveal what you think their silence means and then, switcheroo, they can just change their explanation. . . . Their shell game is as bad as "I'm thinking of a number between one and ten." Whatever you guess, they can claim they were thinking of a different number.[7]*

In other words, silence can be a very good tactic to set up a bait and switch, just as the competitor in Scenario #1 used it.

The body language of silence/compliance is one of composure, with active listening posture enhancing the invitation for the other person to speak. Leaning toward the person to suggest being attentive says, "Talk to me," without saying anything.

A "bait-and-switch" opening is often provocative. Nick shocked his opponent with this declaration he would "steal." The goal is to verbally reel in the other person, assess the situation, and determine the right moment to move in a different direction. This is the technique of a well-prepared individual, someone with a plan to achieve a specific outcome.

The body language of someone effecting a bait-and-switch operation needs to be open and invitational. The person needs to look trustworthy, otherwise the plan won't work if the other person is even slightly observant. On the other hand, the body language of an ideal target would exhibit vulnerability and some measure of stress.

CHAPTER 8

. . . .

MEETINGS

Scheduled meetings give you an advantage to respond verbally and in writing that job interviews, negotiations, sales encounters, and social interactions generally do not. They give you an opportunity to prepare your remarks relative to an agenda, and they present the opportunity to take notes in an efficient, effective, and accurate way. You should know who will be asking you questions and what those questions are likely to address.

In any encounter, when you have more "knowns" than "unknowns," you are well-positioned to use your skill set to control the conversation. As a reminder, that does not mean you do all the talking. In fact, it often means that you do most of the listening and insert your well-phrased responses at a time of your choosing. Never underestimate the power of listening well! (And please note the advice in Chapter 5 on keywords and body language signals.)

In a preponderance of cases, when you participate in a business meeting, you have no excuse for inferior responses to questions and no excuse for second-rate meeting reports—as long as you know about the meeting in advance. We will address those dreaded "spontaneous" meetings later in the chapter.

THE NATURE OF MEETINGS

In theory, the purpose of a meeting is that it's a collaborative tool; it's the *process* to get something done with input from multiple participants. The point of the meeting is to address an issue or set of issues: that's the *content*. Regardless of whether it's a face-to-face event or conducted electronically, unless human beings know how to manage the process, no matter how important the content is, the meeting could be a waste of time. And just because the delivery medium or platform for distance conferencing allows individuals to avoid traveling does not mean that it is inherently more efficient. In fact, if the same group of people can't move toward a common goal in a room together, they will probably have even less focus and efficiency in an electronic meeting.

First, we'll focus on using good questioning and response techniques to keep the content on track, and then we will look at how your responses and body language can support a worthwhile process.

Content

Relatively speaking, managing content is the easy part of the meeting equation. You are entering a situation in which the information you have in your hands and in your head, combined with what you learn at the meeting, have the potential to give you control in the conversation. Let's look at a real example of failure to do this and how to turn the content failure around.

Thomas attended every quarterly meeting of his technical standards organization for thirteen years. It was a record among his peers, all of whom were experts in various areas of electrical engineering. The meeting room for the group was always set up the same way—a large *U* shape consisting of multiple long tables. Thomas always took the same seat at the far-left end of the table. Given the consistency of the room setup, it always put him closest to the rear door of the room and farthest away from the organization's chair, Donna—nicknamed "Chair for Life"—with whom he had a stilted relationship.

Donna would ask Thomas the same question she posed to other delegates with a standard in process: "Where are we with this?" Even though he knew he wasn't answering an actual "place" question, Thomas would commonly say, "At a dead end," or "The middle of nowhere." Donna would roll her eyes and begin to grill him as he came back with monosyllabic responses: "How long until the comment period is over?" "How many comments did you get?" "How many were negative?" "What did they say?" "What other companies are participating?" And so on.

Donna had not mastered the art of questioning, and Thomas had not even begun to cultivate the art of responding. As a result, he felt badgered by her. His job depended on his participation in the organization, so four times a year, he couldn't avoid her.

No one had the optimism to think that Donna and Thomas would ever be friendly, but a consultant was able to lay down some rules that supported less contentious and more content-focused communication. The path to a turnaround for Donna involved reconstructing questions when she addressed Thomas. For Thomas, it centered on four windows on his laptop screen.

Donna learned to ask questions like, "What's occurred with the development of the standard since the last meeting, Thomas?" A keyword like "development" immediately suggests that a narrative is being requested.

Thomas learned to turn to his laptop, and instead of shooting back a glib answer, say, "Let me look at my notes." Just doing that was like hitting a pause button for the meeting. It established Thomas as the center of focus in the room. And instead of having rapid-fire exchanges in which his content was spit out, there was a clean setup to present it coherently.

As you would probably guess, the four windows were pages devoted to each of the four areas of disclosure. This methodology is a potentially life-changing one for someone like Thomas, a highly technical person who felt uncomfortable with the people-related aspects the organization. The four-windows approach helped him organize his thinking to deliver a comprehensive response. He could move smoothly from a "thing" response about events that occurred such as meetings, comments, and revisions to "people" information—who participated, who helped with revisions, and so on. Then, he noted meeting locations, indicating what companies felt committed enough to the standard to host working sessions. He concluded with the timeline of development and projected date of completion.

Applying the disclosure-area approach to note-taking is the preparatory step that precedes a presentation like this. It's what Jim taught his interrogation and law enforcement students who ultimately would be meeting with prisoners of war or people accused of crimes, respectively. Professionals in those capacities have to know when they walk out of the room that they can hand their notes to people who are supposed to act on them. Taking notes sequentially, the way meeting minutes are generally recorded, would never allow them to do that. That model does not help anyone who must be content and result focused.

Jim calls linear note-taking the biblical approach: When you have to refer to them later to create a meaningful report, you are engaged in a time-consuming "seek and ye shall find" (Matthew 7:7) exercise. To best prepare yourself to deliver useful content

at a meeting, do not take notes of remarks and discoveries as they occur. Segregate your information
when you get it into the four disclosure areas—just
like a good interrogator.

People	Places	Things	Time

Process

When you go into a meeting, think of yourself as a
people manager. Particularly, someone in Donna's
role—a facilitator with the lead responsibility for
process—must have a good command of things like
group dynamics, spatial relationships, and desired
outcome. It helps if others in the room are aware of
them though, so even if you are not the facilitator,
you can reinforce process by helping to ensure that
no one is dominating the entire conversation or removing himself from participation.

Without a good process to support your contribution of content in a meeting, even the most spot-
on response to a question may be disregarded by
some and heard only partially by others. You have
worked hard to build the quality of your content.
You want to command the attention of people and
drive toward the result you intend. You need the
process of the meeting to support that outcome.

Martin Murphy, president of QuantumMeetings and author of *No More Pointless Meetings*, has provided meetings advice to some of the largest companies based in the United States. For anyone concerned with the process of meetings, he offers a set of questions to promote brainstorming about what factors might be causing their meetings to go off track. If Donna were going to explore these questions, she might do it with the help of her recording secretary, who probably scribbled notes—later scrubbed from the official minutes—about some of these very things:

⬦ How loudly are people speaking?

⬦ Who's talking the most?

⬦ Who's apparently not listening?

⬦ Who's not participating?

⬦ How many are in the meeting?

⬦ Who are they?

⬦ How long is the meeting scheduled to run?

⬦ Are things getting accomplished?[1]

Murphy's questions cover three of the four disclosure areas. To that list, we would add the critical consideration of place: Where is the meeting and how is it set up? This is the aspect of nonverbal communication known as "proxemics." The discussion in Chapter 5 about proximity and space introduced the importance of the concept, but we will explore it more here. Proxemics is an area of study that explores the amount of personal space that people feel is necessary. If they perceive their boundaries are invaded, they feel uncomfortable, possibly defensive, and have a profound need to use barriers to establish separation. Barriers can by physical, such as angling away from someone or putting a laptop between one person and another. When there is no apparent physical option for separation, however, they can be verbal barriers, like fending off questions—using responses as a shield.

Go back to the initial description of Thomas and his position at the *U*-shaped table arrangement. He was at the end and closest to the rear door of the room. He was seated at an eight-foot table that was supposed to accommodate four people. The proximity made him uncomfortable, so staying toward a corner gave him the sense of more space; the proximity to the door increased his comfort level.

This would sound like overanalysis to anyone without the same kind of need for private space. To Thomas, this was important. Having people so close to him was like being thrust into an amusement park experience of bumper cars. He didn't want to be that close to people, and he felt that his colleagues were encroaching on his personal space.

Thomas's need, which he experienced on a reactive level rather than a conscious one, should have been just as important to every person in that room. Most of them didn't mind being crammed together.

Some of them did, and their way of coping was to leave the room periodically, go to the snack table and grab a donut and cup of coffee, or just pull their chairs back from the tables and breathe.

The quality of the meeting process was affected by the way the space was configured. The diagram below shows a typical view of what is considered acceptable proximity in different situations.

When planning a meeting, it would be wise to consider how much the need for personal space can vary, and therefore configure the tables, as well as space in front and in back of the tables, to allow people to establish personal real estate.

In a videoconference, distance from the camera, lighting, and background help you create a

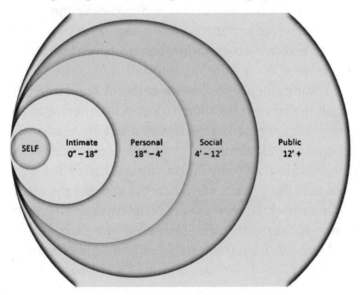

sense of comfortable proximity to others on the call. Jim backlights his computer screen to soften the on-camera image and puts a little distance between himself and the camera, setting himself against a background that is uncluttered and does not steal focus. He should know how to do these things because his experience includes on-camera work for organizations such as Netflix and the Department of Homeland Security.

Another meeting-process consideration—with the focus on seeing yourself as a people manager—is using the psychological levers covered in depth in Chapter 9. To recap and add to the mix, interrogators use a number of manipulative techniques they call "approaches" to get prisoners to talk with them. They have been tested and codified over the years. In other words, their effectiveness in getting people to provide information has been verified many times over.

Their value to you in a meeting is fundamentally no different from their value in an interrogation. They are psychological levers used to encourage people to talk about subjects the questioner deems important. They help build the quality of the process and elicit the content needed to make the meeting worthwhile. Here, we pick up two approaches—arousing curiosity and providing incentives—and add two additional ones: easing fears and certainty.

AROUSING CURIOSITY

Arousing the curiosity of your meeting attendees raises the energy level and gets everyone focused on the same point. Launching a meeting with something provocative can set the tone and pace for the entire session.

Use the Hollywood tactic of teasing the audience with highlights. Your "trailer" could be, "It was a *big* quarter for new contracts! Ask me some questions, and you'll find out how big!"

Another method is to organize your response to a question in reverse order of interest. You are asked, "What happened with contracts this past quarter?" You respond,

Within the past three months, our team of three sales guys and an engineer managed to pull eighteen rabbits out of the hat and score the highest per-quarter number of deals in the history of the company!

Arousing curiosity may require you to be a bit of a PT Barnum at times. We aren't recommending you take a fake mermaid to your meeting, but if you have a twenty-five-inch-tall man, go right ahead.

PROVIDING INCENTIVES

The most common incentive used by meeting organizers is snacks because if you have doughnuts, you have friends. The downside is that many of us have come to expect snacks at meetings so instead of being an incentive, they are an anticipated source of sugar—and nothing more than a reason to get up and walk to the other end of the room to temporarily remove yourself from the meeting.

An example of incentive with purpose is a guest presenter either at the beginning of a meeting or at the end. This piggybacks on the "arousing curiosity" approach because people at the meeting should want to know why the guest speaker is there and what she has to offer. If the guest speaker is Anna from accounting, just make sure that Anna has proven she can make spreadsheets fascinating.

Another incentive is a simple matter of organization. If people who come to your meetings know that you don't push through scheduled breaks or try to work through lunch, they will have an inducement to stay alert and involved while they are in the room. In cautioning against the lengthened sessions, Christopher "The Toy Guy" Byrne notes in his book *Funny Business,* "Think back to how rotten in was in school when gym or recess got cancelled."[2]

EASING FEARS

Mitigating or removing the fear of someone at your meeting can go a long way toward keeping the energy strong and eliminating a major distraction. For example, if the agenda requires someone to report on a project that is in trouble, depending on circumstances, you might want to find a way to soften the experience. If you choose to do that, tell the person at the outset what action you intend to take. Having someone sitting in a meeting with his heart racing and head pounding removes him from the collaborative process; he's far too self-focused to be a fully functioning member of the team.

CERTAINTY

This is based on something interrogators call the "we know all" approach. It involves projecting certainty about the subject you're asking about. The person you are questioning or inviting to speak should therefore talk openly and comprehensively. In theory, whatever he omits, you will cover anyway.

In an interrogation setting, the idea is to convince the prisoner that you already know the location and size of his unit, for example, so he might as well discuss it with you. In a meeting, the approach could simply be the additional encouragement someone needs to provide a complete response to your question.

Using a regulator like nodding your head and other active listening movements would serve as additional encouragement for him to keep talking.

Spontaneous Meetings

When the boss sends out a red alert and calls everyone into the conference room, it's usually to discuss something that requires urgent attention. General guidelines to help you contribute quality content and support a smooth process include the following:

◇ Always walk in with the ability to take notes. Grab paper, a laptop, or whatever you need, but don't go in empty-handed.

◇ Use the four-disclosure area model to take notes. It is highly likely that there will be a discussion of "who will do what," and you want to have those people listed in one place and associated with the correct tasks. Similarly, if this is urgent business, then the timeline for getting tasks done is critical.

◇ Never hesitate to say, "Let me look at my notes" or "I need to think about that for a minute" before responding. One sign that your cognitive brain is in control rather than your limbic system is the ability to approach a problem or request at a thoughtful pace.

EXERCISES

Are You the Best You Can Be?

People commonly prepare for presentations and interviews by investing more than the usual amount of thought into dress and behavior. In contrast, going to a meeting with people you have seen many times before may not involve the same amount of personal preparation. This first exercise is designed to raise your awareness of your own baseline, that is, the movements and voice you rely on when you are in a relatively relaxed state—the way you would probably be in a team or staff meeting.

Do a video/audio recording of yourself carrying on a conversation. Make sure it includes questions and answers from both of you. Ideally, do this exercise with a colleague and link the discussion to your business.

When you watch the video, determine all the elements of your baseline; pay particular attention to your illustrators and adaptors, as well as the vocal traits that characterize your normal, relaxed speech.

Show the video to someone with whom you've sat in meetings. If you have a strong relationship with your boss and consider him or her a mentor, that would be an ideal person to view the recording.

Ask yourself, and that person, two questions:

◇ From a content perspective, what could I do better/differently to get my points across?

◇ From a body language perspective, what in my repertoire of movements enhances perceptions of me, and what could be improved or eliminated?

What's Different About You?

Attire is part of a person's body language, so it's sending nonverbal signals. Reading those signals can promote more positive energy in a group.

If you're attending a meeting with a group of lawyers and one of them walks in with a leather NASCAR jacket over his suit, he is making a statement. He knows he's different from other people in the room and wants to call attention to his uniqueness. You could say the same for a woman who accessorizes with exotic jewelry or an executive who always wears gold cuff links in the shape of airplanes. People making such distinctive statements are inviting your notice; giving them attention has the potential to improve the dynamics of the group. By simply noticing them, you are conveying, "Hey, I think that's interesting. Tell me more."

Look around at people you have meetings with periodically, and see if anything about their attire stands out—and represents a consistent part of their presentation. It could be the color of their eyeglasses or tendency to wear colorful scarves. This is the kind of observation you can make regardless of whether your meetings are face-to-face or video conferences.

Express curiosity about it to the person. "Where do you get those colorful scarves?" or "What is the significance of those cuff links?" has no inherent flattery associated with it, so if you hate them, you aren't being fake. That fact that you exhibit curiosity says something more important. It says, "I'm interested in learning more about you."

If you're okay with doing this—this is not a time to step way outside your comfort zone—wear something to a meeting that, normally, only friends

would see on you. Make a mental note of who noticed and asked you about it and how that made
you feel.

Maryann did this on one occasion when she was
a consultant going into an intense meeting about
raising money for a health-care project. She deliberately wore two different earrings. The client con-
ducting the meeting suddenly noticed and interject-
ed, "Did you mean to wear two different earrings or
was that a mistake?" Maryann replied, "I did it on
purpose." "Oh, how creative!" she said, and when
on with the meeting. Everyone had a laugh, and the
tone of the meeting was a little lighter after that.

It's not about the earrings. It's about the energy
in the room changing when people pay more attention to each other.

CHAPTER 9

. . . .

MEDIA INTERVIEWS

Before a long radio interview on a book about sex after cancer that she wrote with a physician,[1] Maryann got a set of ten questions she would be asked during the broadcast. She was working on this book at the time and made a concerted effort to prepare for the interview by crafting answers covering all four subject areas. One example is: "How did you go about researching this topic?"

> We spent a weekend brainstorming and then created a detailed outline for the book and a plan to finish the research in three months. We listed every issue we thought readers would want this book to cover—from psychotherapy to sex toys. Then we made a list of relevant experts as well as patients who had heart-wrenching and heart-warming stories. We focused on patients we could sit with face-to-face, so they would be comfortable sharing their thoughts on the impact of their cancer diagnosis and treatment on intimacy.

People: coauthors, experts, patients, readers
Things: outline, plan, issues, psychotherapy, sex toys, stories, cancer, intimacy
Time: a weekend, three months
Place: face-to-face

Note: This was a "soft" interview, in that the host of the broadcast was looking for how-to guidance for her listeners, as well as the background that shaped the insights and techniques the book covered. Her agenda was providing listeners with information they could act on, trusting the authority of the authors and not putting them on the spot for the advice in the book or probing their sources.

Having no idea what type of media interview you might be facing, we crafted the advice in this chapter to apply to news and features-oriented interviews.

THE NATURE OF MEDIA QUESTIONS

Professional journalists learn questioning skills and can tell you easily why things like repeat, persistent, and summary questions are essential to their work. They seek a complete answer with as many of the four subject areas covered as is reasonable. We are not including people without experience and credentials in this group, by the way. People who have posted stories online but have never been trained or paid to investigate and write stories for news organizations are not the breed we are discussing.

We are talking about professionals whose job it is to inform with facts and to seek accountability. Ironically, many easy questions from the mouths of journalists are construed as tough simply because the respondent knows the reporter seeks accountability.

Before providing guidance on responding to media questions, it's useful to know what aspiring journalists are told about how to do their job.

How They Ask

In brief, here is what someone teaching a journalism course focused on the art of the interview (also known as asking questions) might consist of:

⬧ Know as much as possible about the topic of the interview or the person being interviewed before you pose questions. Verify with the interviewee whatever information you brought to the interview to ensure it is accurate and current. Do not assume that websites or social media are reliable sources.

⬧ Ask questions until you feel you have the information you need. Sometimes you must ask the same question several different ways.

⬧ Try to keep questions specific and concise. If you do not digress, the likelier it is that the interviewee will stay on topic.

◇ One of the advantages of an interview via email is that questions and answers are in black and white and free of interruptions that can sidetrack people. Just be sure you know who is supplying the answers. One of the disadvantages of an email interview is that you cannot observe the person who is answering the question. You can neither verify that the person answering is who owns the emails address. Another is that you also miss information that a person's appearance and body language provide.

◇ Do not hesitate to ask the same question until it is answered to your satisfaction, to admit you don't fully understand a topic, or to ask the interviewee to slow down, repeat and/or speak in nontechnical terms. Lawyers, politicians, and scientists tend to be use trade jargon that may be unclear to the public.

◇ Above all, observe, listen, and take a lot of notes. Don't be preoccupied with the next question you are going to ask, thereby missing the answer that is given. The objective is to gain knowledge, not impart it.

Question Enhancers

Experienced interrogators like Jim have a lot in common with journalists: They both want their questions answered sooner rather than later.

Whether they are aware of it or not, the most skilled journalists use psychological levers to help get the job done. These tools to get people to talk are no different from what interrogators call "approaches," which are studied and used deliberately with prisoners. Not all approaches are transferrable to the process of getting information from a non-prisoner, but these are:

AROUSING CURIOSITY

Broadcast journalists often have a daily challenge of questioning guests they hope to engage while sustaining the curiosity of audience members. They want people hearing the exchange to crave the next question and response. When the broadcasters get it right, they utilize a powerful determinant of curiosity, that is, the intensity with which people want to resolve their uncertainly about an issue.

All journalists also have the challenge of asking good enough questions of interviewees that they also have curiosity about what the next question is.

PROVIDING INCENTIVES

An outrageous example of a media interview centering on an incentive occurred in 2005, when Brad Pitt was promoting the film *Mr. and Mrs. Smith*. He agreed to have an hour-long chat with Diane Sawyer about subjects the public deeply cared about—his breakup with his wife and rumored affair with his costar—if part of the time could be spent focusing on poverty in Africa. Although it isn't likely that someone will get you to talk with outrageous incentives like that, you may be offered a lunch or a latte. You may also be offered something intangible such as information about a competitor or a situation of interest. A reputable journalist would not do this, so your alarms should go off if an incentive becomes part of the interview package.

APPEALING TO EMOTIONS

A journalist can emotionally appeal to an expert simply by highlighting the value of the person's information to readers or listeners. A feel-good motive, however, is not the most powerful kind of emotional driver. If a reporter can arouse anger, disgust, or pain, he's exercising much greater force over the person's desire to answer questions.

There are effective and ineffective ways to do this, of course. Some of the journalists lobbing questions at the 2015–2016 debates among US presidential candidates did it well. On numerous occasions, they got candidates rattled enough to keep them talking about hot-button issues.

There are also plenty of examples when strong emotions were aroused without that being the intent. For example, after Hurricane Harvey devastated Houston, CNN sent reporters to a shelter to interview evacuees. One reporter who seemed to lack the sensitivity required by the situation interviewed a mother who had been stranded with her children waiting for help for thirty-six hours. She aroused emotion—a lot more than she expected:

And you really trying to understand with the microphone still in my face? With me shivering cold, with my kids wet, and you still putting the microphone in my face.[2]

Anytime you arouse another person's emotions, whether you are the questioner or responder, you are dealing with a person whose cognitive abilities are diminished. The more emotions overtake the person, the less likely it is the person can have a well-reasoned exchange with you.

The physiological reality of arousing emotion is that the person slips into a limbic state of reactivity. Cognitive abilities are diminished, even though the person may seem really on top of things. Particularly if someone is in survival mode, whether physical or psychological, the person enters a fight-flight-or-freeze state with autonomic nervous system functions overtaking cognitive ones.

On the positive side, as in the presidential debates, when the candidates leak emotions, they can lose just enough control to show their true colors.

BOOSTING EGO

Flattery works. Research indicates that even insincere flattery works. If you hear phrases like, "It's such an honor" and "Your insights on that were inspiring," aren't you inclined to want to answer the person's questions?

Scientific American began its January 12, 2010 article entitled "Flattery Will Get You Far" with this paragraph:

> *Here at Scientific American we understand the wisdom of our readership. Your intellect sets you apart from the rest of the population, and . . . as someone of exceptional judgment, we know you will be interested in subscribing to our exclusive online material . . . available to you for only $9.99/month.*[3]

Despite your possible skepticism, insincere flattery like this works—time after time. In 2010, researchers at the Hong Kong University of Science and Technology published a paper in the *Journal of Marketing Research* entitled "Insincere Flattery Actually Works: A Dual Attitudes Perspective."[4] Their paper probes when and how flattery makes people more positive about and cooperative with the source of compliments.

Elaine Chan and Jaideep Sengupta asked their study participants to rely solely on an advertisement to evaluate the merits of a new department store. The ad essentially praised readers for their discerning taste and implied that is what would bring them to the store. The critical aspect of this manipulation is that readers were aware of the ploy. On a conscious level, they knew they were being played—but flattery still influenced their behavior. Their positive attitudes toward the store prevailed. Chan and Sengupta concluded that "the flattery was exerting an important effect outside their awareness."[5]

DEFLATING EGO

Going back to the presidential debates, journalists used this approach when they targeted logic gaps and blatant misrepresentations in a candidate's previous statements. Done well, as in some of these instances, it helps the reporter live up to the responsibility to seek accountability. The interviewee feels duly challenged and responds with a more comprehensive answer than if no one had probed more deeply. Done poorly, it alienates the individual and arouses antagonism. Instead of eliciting answers, the questioner sets up the interviewee for a counterattack.

RESPONDING TO MEDIA

You will be responding to question types we labeled "good" in Chapter 2, as well as those we classified as "bad," meaning that the question is not phrased so that you are clear on what's being asked. You will also field questions that fit our criteria for "easy," and those we've called "tough." The guidance provided previously that relates to all of them applies here. The big difference is that your responses in a meeting might not go beyond the walls of the conference room, whereas your exchange with a media professional could go around the world in a matter of seconds. Taking time to think before speaking is a good general rule.

Answering Bad Questions

Even people who ask questions for a living make mistakes in constructing questions—and sometimes they are essentially forced into making them. One example is a presidential press conference in which each White House reporter might get one shot at asking a question. If that's the case, the reporter will seize the opportunity to stuff multiple questions into one long one. Compound questions dominate press conferences, so most presidents get good at tearing them into their component parts and responding.

Don't be offended if you get a compound question. Do what the POTUS does and take it apart first.

⬧ You are asked: "How did you make this discovery, and what significance will it have for health care in the next five years?"

⬧ You respond: "First, I'll explain how I made the discovery, and then, I'll speculate on the effects it might have on health care."

Be wary of leading questions. If you are asked a question that contains an inherent judgment, repeat it without the embedded foregone conclusion and answer your "clean" question.

⬧ You are asked: "How bad do you feel that your last book was ignored by the *Chicago Tribune*?"

◇ You respond: "You are asking how I feel about the lack of coverage in my home-town newspaper . . ."

Similarly, be wary of negative questions. Again, the tactic is to restate it in such a way that it is clear what you are thinking; that's more important than the lack of clarity in the question. Negative questions tend to be unplanned in the sense that the reporter knows what information he wants, but he hasn't thought through how to express the request.

◇ You are asked: "Have you never stopped, or never not cared, about the level of poverty in that part of Africa?"

◇ You respond: "I understand you want to know about my continuing commitment to addressing poverty in Africa."

Vague questions are also a likely outcome of the person not thinking through how to express a desire for certain information. Your goal is to target the fact or opinion that the reporter wants and provide it.

◇ You are asked: "Given the mixed opinions about the value of cryptocurrency, we have heard a whole spectrum of statements about valuation. What do you think?"

◇ You respond: "Are you asking me if I think Bitcoin is worth anything?"

Technically, yes-or-no questions when a narrative response is desired makes them bad questions.

Practically speaking, though, we all ask these questions and hope the interviewee responds with a complete thought. A week after the Marjory Stoneman Douglas High School shooting in February 2018, a surviving student on his way to the White House to meet with President Donald Trump was asked the following by an excellent NPR reporter, who had sincerely expressed empathy in the course of the interview: "Is there something you want him to say?" The high school senior understood fully that she wanted more than a "yes" or "no" in response—and so did every listener. Although a better phrasing would have been, "What would you like to hear from the president?" anyone following the report knew what she was after.

◇ If asked a yes-or-no question, you have the option of saying "yes" or "no" or "maybe."

◇ You also have the option of providing a narrative response and completely bypassing the yes-or-no part. If the reporter wants the definitive answer, then it's up to her to ask you the question again.

Nonanswers

Agreeing to speak with media professionals means that you are willing to help them do their job, that is, you are willing and able to answer questions. Nonetheless, you may still be faced with questions you cannot answer or don't know how to answer. Instead of giving a completely empty response like "no comment," legitimately add at least one of the four subject areas to the nonanswer. Use connectors such as "because" or "however" to allow yourself to be more informative.

◇ I have no comment at the moment, however, I may be able to respond at another time.

◇ I have no comment, but you might pose that question to John Doe at EPA.

◇ I have no comment because of confidentiality issues.

If you don't know the answer, try to be more helpful than, "I don't know."

◇ I don't know, but John Doe at EPA might.

◇ I don't know right now, but I'll try to find out by tomorrow.

◇ I don't know anything about that study, however, we are doing a related environmental impact statement. Would you like information on that?

◇ I don't know where that occurred; I'm based in Washington, DC, and this happened in the field.

Managing Question Enhancers

Review the psychological levers we described. Each can generate an atmosphere and mood that is potentially beneficial to your interaction with the journalist.

They also could make the questioning more difficult than it needs to be.

AROUSING CURIOSITY

A well-structured interview is potentially a lively conversation between two well-informed people. The journalist has done her homework; questions are rooted in facts. That said, do not assume that a reporter will avoid bringing up rumors as well. Consider that a question being asked by reporter probably means it has already being posed on social media. The best course is to address it rather than to ignore it and appear to be hiding something.

Respect the fact that rumors can spark a great deal of curiosity, and your role in the scenario is to satisfy that curiosity with information.

PROVIDING INCENTIVES

You don't have to say no to the coffee as long as it's not spiked. With sometimes hilarious results, *The Graham Norton Show* supplies guests with alcohol if they want it. It's an incentive that has gotten more than one celebrity pouring out answers to questions that weren't even asked.

Another type of incentive is the quid pro quo, in which the journalist offers something like "insider information" or a candid fact about himself in the hope that you return the favor. Used appropriately, the quid pro quo does nothing more than reinforce the trust that's building between the two people in the conversation. It can be pushed over the line, however, so understand there is no inherent obligation to divulge any of your secrets.

APPEALING TO EMOTIONS

Certain words and concepts will trigger an emotional response from most people. If words like "outrageous," "repulsive," and "tragic" make their way into a question, a little alarm should go off that warns you the question conveys negative emotions. Listen for the modifiers in any question and mentally try to strip them out.

You might try repeating the portion of the question without the modifier. For example, you're a civil engineer and a reporter asks for your expert response to the deadly bridge collapse: "The bridge collapse occurred because . . ."

BOOSTING EGO

Say thank you to the compliment and move on to answering the question.

DEFLATING EGO

In fielding a legitimately challenging question from a reporter that could cause discomfort or embarrassment, the first thing to do is get clarity on it. Be certain you know what the person is asking, and then make a decision about whether or not you wish to respond.

Remember that reporters are trained to be skeptical, partly because they are bombarded with unsolicited stories by people who are pushing a product or idea. You will be a good partner in quality reporting by being just as skeptical about both information and questions that arise in the course of your media interview.

CHAPTER 10
. . . .
SOCIAL INTERACTIONS

Superman can fly even if he's wearing street clothes. He doesn't lose the ability to do it when he hangs up his cape in a closet; he chooses not to do it. You can make the same choice about when and where to use your new skills. Just keep in mind that everything we've shared with you in this book can be a force for good.

When people find out that we focus on interpersonal skills, they commonly miss the force-for-good potential and ask, "Do you use this stuff on your friends and family?" The misperception is that knowing a lot about body language, questioning techniques, and controlling a conversation makes you a manipulative individual. It can; however, when you use these interpersonal skills with family or other people with whom you have social interactions, the intent is to enrich communication, not to dominate or distort it.

In this final chapter, we focus on social situations in looking at ways to enhance your understanding of what other people mean when they ask you a question, and how your response makes them feel. There are cultural nuances, regional differences in speech, and changes in both the connotation and denotation of words that can cause confusion. Using textual analysis and reading body language, you can get even greater clarity than you already have on what is being asked and how best to respond.

Cognitive psychologist and linguist Steven Pinker explains that when two people use language to help them interact socially, they are requiring language to operate on two levels—expecting their words to do two different jobs. His insight helps illuminate the importance of analyzing cultural nuances and word choices, and having that knowledge affect how you pose and respond to questions:

> *We use language at two levels: the literal form signals the safest relationship with the listener, whereas the implicated content—the reading between the lines that we count on the listener to perform—allows the listener to derive the interpretation which is most relevant in context, which possibly initiates a changed relationship.*[1]

For example, you could say "If you hand me that bottle of water, I'd appreciate it." The person complies by handing you the water; it's understood in context as an imperative, but it comes across as a polite request. When it's a question—"Would you please hand me that bottle of water?"—compliance is probably verbalized as "Sure" and then the person hands you the water. The question takes the imperative quality up a notch, but it still comes across as a polite request. "Hand me that bottle of water," is an order, however, and compliance with it establishes momentary dominance of the person requesting the water.

TEXTUAL ANALYSIS

Knowing something about textual analysis should make you more forgiving, not more judgmental, about how and why people pose the questions they do. An academic explanation of textual analysis is that it's "a way for researchers to gather information about how other human beings make sense of the world."[2] And what is the "text" in textual analysis?

> What exactly is a text? Answer: whenever we produce an interpretation of something's meaning—a book, television program, film, magazine, T-shirt or kilt, piece of furniture or ornament—we treat it as a text. A text is something that we make meaning from.[3]

Let's look at the not-so-academic application of textual analysis in terms of how you understand and respond to a question.

People all over the world have exposure to American television, which theoretically gives viewers a peek at American culture (if there is such a thing). Imagine you were a German high school student in 2015. You are thinking about coming to the United States the summer after your graduation, so you're watching American shows to get a better feel for what it's like in US cities. That student might have discovered America by watching *CSI: Crime Scene Investigation, NCIS, Bones, CSI: Cyber, NCIS: Los Angeles, The Blacklist, Hawaii Five-0, Criminal Minds, The Mentalist,* and *The Mysteries of Laura.*[4] According to *Vulture*, which specializes in entertainment news, those were the top ten US shows in Germany in 2015. That same year, Americans were probably perceived as much more benevolent and playful in Brazil where *Kung Fu Panda* and *SpongeBob SquarePants* were among the shows that dominated in popularity.[5]

Value judgments would be associated with the perceptions gathered from these different kinds of programs, as well as a determination of how realistic or unrealistic the representation of Americans is in each of the shows. The best response to the same question from that young German visitor and a recent US high school graduate might therefore be different.

In addition, some words and concepts do not translate from one language/culture to another. Here are some examples of words with no direct English translations provided in a *Huffington Post* article:

Schadenfreude
Language: German
Meaning: A feeling of enjoyment that comes from seeing or hearing about the troubles of other people

Hygge
Language: Danish
Meaning: The act of relaxing with loved ones and good friends, usually while enjoying food and drink; the word is associated with coziness.[6]

Regardless of whether a cultural difference is the reason, on a day-to-day basis, you are likely to encounter challenges of words causing confusion because the questioner or responder is relying on a denotation rather than connotation, or vice versa. For example, you are at a dinner party and guests are gathered in the living room before the meal is served. One guest says very cheerily, "There is quite an odor in the kitchen!" A remark like that would probably send the hostess racing toward the kitchen to find out what was burning. By definition, "odor" means a distinctive smell, but nearly everyone fluent in English recognizes it as a word describing an unpleasant smell.

An even more common mistake is misuse of words like "notoriety," "tortuous," and "kudos." How would you respond to a question like this: "How much notoriety did you achieve by writing that book with the interrogator?" Technically, you are being asked how well known you became after committing the despicable act of writing a book with an interrogator. Notoriety is the fame of felons and people who throw tomatoes at nuns.

Watch and listen for words with meanings that have become inverted as well, or that a particular region uses differently from what you're accustomed to. The word "terrific" had a seriously negative connotation when we were growing up, but commonly, it is used now to say, "Wow! That's great!" And in New England, you might hear something referred to as "wicked good." In that context, "wicked" has nothing to do with evil.

Whether the offending remark was about an odor in your kitchen or your notoriety as an author, your analysis of the context and usage should lead you to conclude that no harm was meant. Don't correct the person's word choice; respond to the question that she intended to ask or the remark she thought she was making. At that point, you are utilizing the second level of Pinker's explanation of language: "[It] allows the listener to derive the interpretation which is most relevant in context."

BETTER UNDERSTANDING THROUGH BODY LANGUAGE

Consistent with the spirit of understanding engendered by textual analysis, we want to remind you of the insights in Chapter 5 on exhibiting openness in your body language. The basics are avoiding movements that close off your body in the front, refraining from nervous gestures, minimizing barriers between you and another person, and using active listening to encourage conversation.

In a social situation, you may see indications of both open and closed body language that don't show up in a professional environment—at least not the same way. Here are a few things to look for:

CHANGE IN PLACEMENT OF A GLASS OR PLATE

In a social situation, it is common for people just getting acquainted to use barriers such as a drinking glass or plate of appetizers to separate themselves from another person. The couple in the photo probably just met or don't know each other well. Without even realizing it, they are using their glasses to create a bit of separation.

When the individual looks for a place to set that plate down or move the wine glass from in front of her to the side, that is a display of increased comfort with you. The converse would not necessarily be true, though. It's possible that someone with a growing level of comfort about conversing with you also has a growing level of comfort about eating in front of you. Don't necessarily interpret the sudden appearance of a plate of cheese as an attempt to create distance.

Sticking out a tongue

Zoologist Desmond Morris thought that humans stick out their tongues as a sign of rejection. His premise is observation of primate infants who stick out their tongue against a mother's breast to indicate, "No more." When it's done spontaneously, as opposed to deliberately, construe it as a negative response to whatever you just said.

Leaning in or out

In a professional environment, you will probably see mirroring, but not a pronounced leaning in to each other. You might also experience the opposite. Maryann was once in the bar area of a restaurant intentionally observing people for a previous book on body language and watched a young man go from leaning toward his date on the other side of the table to sitting straight up, to leaning back, to tipping his chair back. He could not get any further away from her unless he fell over or got up and walked away.

As with leaning in and out, there is likely to be less subtlety on angling in a social situation than there is in a professional one. Depending on how people are mixing and mingling, a person might even be able to get away with turning her back to someone she had just been talking to. There are graceful ways to transition from one person to another, and that is not one of them. The opposite could also occur as you find yourself the one who now has the full attention of another person in a crowded room.

After all of the learning and practicing you've done in the course of these ten chapters, you are you going to be much more effective responding to questions than you were before. Yet, because you are dealing with language, it's impossible to get it right all the time. No matter how thoughtfully and artfully we choose our words, we are dealing with an inevitable fluidity in meaning and usage. Pinker notes:

> *The vagueness of language, far from being a bug or an imperfection, actually might be a feature of language, one that we use to our advantage in social interactions.*[7]

Pinker's words should remind us that the value of getting better at questioning and responding to questions is to use language to help us understand each other better. Yes, if your skill exceeds the other person's, you can control the conversation in the sense that you can moderate and direct it. By no means is that synonymous with diminishing the importance of the other person's contributions, however. Instead, you are engaged in a coordinated movement with language: One person leads, one person follows, and both are dancing.

EXERCISE

We told you in the introduction we would come back to this! Now that you have a firm grasp of the distinction between answering and responding to a question—now that you have a new skill set to control a conversation—we are inviting you to answer the initial four questions again.

Please pull out the answers you wrote down before. Now create new ones using the skill set you acquired.

⬦ Where were you on a memorable New Year's Eve?

⬦ Who is your grandfather on your mother's side?

⬦ What is your favorite restaurant?

⬦ How did you celebrate your birthday last year?

To conclude, we will expose a little bit of ourselves by providing our answers.

Where were you on a memorable New Year's Eve?

Jim:

New Year's Eve 1963, my brothers and I took my mom's pans and lids into the backyard of our duplex apartment in Paramount, California, and beat the thunder out of them at midnight—and boy, were we in trouble! For the rest of my life in that home, none of those pan lids fit. Every time we used them, it reminded me of that night.

Maryann:

December 31, 1999, I flew back to San Francisco from Washington, DC, and nearly fainted into my bed from a horrible case of flu. Being a Prince lover, I heard his 1999 in my head as I blew my nose. Four days later, I had champagne.

Who is your grandfather on your mother's side?

Jim:

He was William Owen Bagby of Pike County, Illinois, but everybody called him Stump—and he told us grandkids why. He said he was a long way from home one night and a thunderstorm came up. He was running home because he was scared, and right in front of him, a lightning bolt struck a tree stump and split it wide open. As he ran through it, his suspenders caught on it, and he was stuck there until somebody rescued him later that night.

Maryann:

His name was Michael, and he died in a motor-cycle crash on July 3, 1927. He was thirty-seven and my grandmother was twenty-seven with two young children. He played the violin, but that didn't pay the bills, so he worked underground in the ore mines.

What is your favorite restaurant?

Jim:

The Wharf in Old Town Alexandria, Virginia, where my dear wife and I had celebrated many anniversaries because the lobster is so good. To make it even better, we were enjoying ourselves in a 200-year-old building in a town that was home to some of the Founding Fathers of our country.

Maryann:

It's a cozy and superb restaurant called Seasoned in Estes Park, Colorado. The executive chef invited me to be sous chef for a day because he knows that, back in 1994, I made a choice between my first book deal and going into a culinary arts program.

How did you celebrate your birthday last year?

Jim:

My wife and "little rascals" and I cashed in a gift card at a seafood restaurant. My wife gave me a mug that reveals a loving message when hot liquid is poured in it, and my daughters, sick of smelling my old stinky sandals, bought me a new pair.

Maryann:

My sweetheart, Jim, as well as a few dear friends, had dinner at Seasoned, where I later served as sous chef for a day. After the tastiest vegetarian meal I've ever had, I was invited into the kitchen where I would one day be chopping and stirring for a twelve-hour shift.

GLOSSARY

Adaptor: A nervous or self-soothing movement like rubbing your fingers together or stroking your neck. A person who may be uncomfortable about asking or answering a question might use an adaptor. It's a sign of stress.

Barrier: Using a body part or object to put separation between you and another person. The proverbial "cold shoulder" is a barrier. It suggests stress is present.

Baseline: The basis for comparison between what is customary and what is a deviation from customary when observing or listening to someone's response to a question. A person who is usually calm but has a sudden change in voice or movement in responding to a question is deviating from baseline. It's a sign of stress.

Batoning: Using a body part, generally an arm, to emphasize a point. It is a type of "illustrator" that bears a resemblance to a conductor using a baton. In response to a difficult question, a person might use batoning as part of a denial or to drive home a point that he thinks is particularly noteworthy.

Commentator: A commentator is thorough and gives complete answers, in some cases, overly complete in the sense that you get more than you asked for. A commentator may provide such a multifaceted answer that it could take the questioning in a different direction.

Compound question: A question that combines two or more subjects, so you are essentially asking two questions at once. For example, "Are you going home or to the restaurant?"

Control question: A question to which you know the answer already.

Corrective questions: A question your mom, your first grade teacher, or your boss might have asked: "Are you always this lazy?" or "Are you trying to drive me nuts?"

Dictator: Someone who answers definitively. The negative aspect of a dictator's response, which may necessitate further questioning, is that he may present a personal opinion as fact. He may also have just a decisive quality to responses that he can be off-putting, depending on the circumstances.

Direct question: A question that leads with a basic interrogative.

Directive phrases: Phrases meant to present an idea or situation as being obvious; examples are "of course" and "without a doubt."

Elicitation: The technique of steering conversation toward a topic to unearth the information you want; this is not a questioning technique, but rather considered an advanced interrogation technique.

Evader: Someone who tends to sidestep questions may just have an idiosyncratic way of listening and understanding rather than want to avoid answering. Evasion could also mean the person feels uncomfortable answering questions for some reason.

Illustrator: A movement that effectively punctuates what a person is saying. It might be a finger pointing, an arm waving, a head cocked, or any number of other movements that express something about the emotion related to the statement. (Also see "Batoning.")

Integrator: Someone who weighs the best way to answer your question. The person waits to hear how you respond to the answer and then may attempt to clarify the initial response, or may offer multiple answers in a single response so you know the person has considered that there may be several good answers.

Leading question: A question suggesting the answer within the question; for example, "How guilty do you feel about taking that kid's lollipop?"

Limbic mode: Emotions have taken over the mental state; in limbic mode, a person has diminished cognitive ability.

Negative question: A question that integrates negatives such as "never" or "not" so that a person is unclear about the answer. For example, "Do you ever not care about the environment?"

Non-pertinent question: A question that doesn't pertain to the subject you really want to know about, but it's one the person will probably not lie about; it serves the purpose of seeing what the truth "looks like" and getting the person to open up to you. It also may be used to redirect attention away from a stress development or to give the questioner time to make a note or check notes.

Persistent question: The same question repeated and perhaps phrased differently; it's a way to check for the thoroughness and perhaps the accuracy of the information given.

Polite question: A question like, "How are you?"

Prequestion: A non-discovery question that asks permission to ask a question; it's often part of rapport-building.

Regulator: A movement intended to control conversation, like nodding the head as if to say, "Get on with it!"

Repeat question: A question that tries to uncover the same information as a previous question, but it's actually different from the first one. For example, a doctor asks you, "What time did you last have anything to eat or drink?" when you first arrive for your surgery. Just before administering anesthesia, he asks you, "You must be thirsty. How many hours has it been since you've had anything to drink?"

Requestion: A non-discovery question that asks certain responses, usually "yes" or "no," such as "Will you marry me?"

Source lead: Information dropped by the respondent in the course of conversation that the questioner feels there is value in pursuing, that is, an additional person, place, thing, or event may be mentioned that warrants attention. For example, in a job interview, the candidate might thank the interviewer for holding the meeting at nine because he's in a golf tournament that starts at noon; the interviewer would circle back to that to determine whether or not the candidate thinks that golf is more important than work.

Rhetorical question: A question intended to provoke a thought, not a fact-based an answer. For example, "Why do I have a conscience?"

Summary question: A question that is intended to allow the person an opportunity to revisit the answer. You might *frame* the question by repeating what the person said and asking, "How does that match up with want you want in this car?"

Vague question: An indistinct question. For example, "When you went to the grocery store, did it seem like a lot of people might be just wandering around looking for something that appealed to them?"

Notes

Introduction

1. Jason Nazar quoting Wendy Lea in "35 Questions That Will Change Your Life," Forbes, September 5, 2013; *www.forbes.com/sites/jasonnazar/2013/09/05/35-questions-that-will-change-your-life/#6fe24195660e*

Chapter 1

1. Press Conference #796, Executive Office of the President, January 2, 1942, with Franklin Delano Roosevelt; *www.fdrlibrary.marist.edu/_resources/images/pc/pc0128.pdf* Courtesy of the FDR Library, digital collection; *www.fdrlibrary.marist.edu/archives/collections/franklin/?p=collections/findingaid&id=508*

2. "Phoenix to Self: 'Why Am I Talking About This?' . . . Joaquin, Shut Up,'" Fresh Air, January 21, 2014; *www.npr.org/2014/01/21/264524233/phoenix-to-self-why-am-i-talking-about-this-joaquin-shut-up*

3. Ibid.

4. Allison Fass, "10 Characteristics of Really Interesting People," Inc., March 8, 2013; *www.inc.com/allison-fass/jessica-hagy-interesting-people-characteristics.html*

CHAPTER 2

1. Raf Weverbergh and Kristien Vermoesen, "The 35 (!) Techniques Politicians Use to Avoid Answering Interview Questions," FINN; *www.finn.be/blogs/35-techniques-politicians-use-avoid-answering-interview-questions*

2. Laszlo Bock, senior vice president of people operations at Google, as interviewed by Adam Bryant, "In Head-Hunting, Big Data May Not Be Such a Big Deal," *New York Times*, June 19, 2013; *www.nytimes.com/2013/06/20/business/in-head-hunting-big-data-may-not-be-such-a-big-deal.html?pagewanted=all&_r=0*

3. "Ray Charles: The 'Fresh Air' Interview," November 24, 2016; *www.npr.org/2016/11/24/503142478/ray-charles-the-fresh-air-interview*

4. "Decoding the Artful Sidestep," Harvard Business School, *Working Knowledge*, November 17, 2008; *https://hbswk.hbs.edu/item/decoding-the-artful-sidestep*

5. Ibid.

6. Mathew Cole Weiss, "The Greatest Actor Responses to Shi**y Interview Questions," Ranker, *www.ranker.com/list/funny-celebrity-interview-responses/matthewcoleweiss*

Chapter 3

1. Deborah Schroeder-Saulnier, *The Power of Paradox: Harness the Energy of Competing Ideas to Uncover Radically Innovative Solutions* (Pompton Plains, NJ: Career Press, 2014), 24.

2. Todd Rogers and Michael I. Norton, "How Politicians Evade Debate Questions," *New York Times,* October 2, 2012; *www.nytimes.com/roomfordebate/2012/01/22/why-politicians-get-away-with-lying/how-politicians-evade-debate-questions*

3. Paul Smith, *Sell with a Story* (New York, NY: AMACOM Books, 2017), 16–24.

4. Mark Satterfield, *Unique Sales Stories: How to Get More Referrals, Differentiate Yourself from the Competitive & Close More Sales Through the Power of Stories* (Atlanta, GA: Mandalay Press, 2011).

5. Heather Finn, "36 Interview Questions That Are Actually Fun to Answer," *Fast Company,* February 5, 2016; *www.fastcompany.com/3056142/36-interview-questions-that-are-actually-fun-to-answer*

Chapter 4

1. "Opinion Words and Phrases," Scholastic, *www.scholastic.com/content/dam/teachers/blogs/genia-connell/migrated-files/opinion_words_and_phrases.pdf*

2. Jim McCormick and Maryann Karinch, *Body Language Sales Secrets: How to Read Prospects and Decode Subconscious Signals to Get Results and Close the Deal* (Wayne, NJ: Career Press, 2017), 129.

Chapter 5

1. Carrie Johnson, "Rachel Brand, Third in Command at the Justice Department, Is Leaving Her Post," National Public Radio, February 9, 2018; *www.npr.org/people/127410674/carrie-johnson*

2. Wade Roush, "What's the Best Q&A Site?" *MIT Technology Review,* December 22, 2006; *www.technologyreview.com/s/407029/whats-the-best-qa-site/*

3. Justin Wm. Moyer and Jenny Starrs, "Bernie Sanders Wags His Finger a Lot, and People Are Starting to Talk About It," *Washington Post,* February 12, 2016; *www.washingtonpost.com/news/morning-mix/wp/2016/02/12/bernie-sanders-wags-his-finger-a-lot-and-people-are-starting-to-talk-about-it/?utm_term=.880764b2c316*

4. Daniel O'Callahan, "Big Bang Theory on Body Language," YouTube, *www.youtube.com/watch?v=vicuZS0ChYQ*

Chapter 6

1. *Fox News Sunday with Chris Wallace,* January 14, 2018; *www.foxnews.com/on-air/fox-news-sunday-chris-wallace/*

2. Laurie Kulikowski, "10 Tech Companies with the Highest Paying Sales Jobs," *TheStreet,* July 17, 2015; *www.thestreet.com/story/13221534/1/10-tech-companies-with-the-highest-paying-sales-jobs.html*

Chapter 7

1. "Million Dollar Microsecond," RadioLab, WNYC, February 4, 2018; *www.radiolab.org/story/267195-million-dollar-microsecond/*

2. Ibid.

3. Ibid.

4. Ibid.

5. Matthew Kirdahy, "CEOs Who Appear in Their Own Commercials," Forbes, April 22, 2008; *www.forbes.com/2008/04/22/ceo-corporate-image-lead-manage-cx_mk_0421tv_slide_12.html#702b0d0e1dbd*

6. "Vintage Ads: Perdue Chickens—Tender Chicken," YouTube, *www.youtube.com/watch?v=uN37i9qr0zY*

7. Jeremy E. Sherman, "The Silent Treatment: When People Leave You Guessing," Psychology Today, October 25, 2011; *www.psychologytoday.com/blog/ambigamy/201110/the-silent-treatment-when-people-leave-you-guessing*

CHAPTER 8

1. Martin Murphy, *No More Pointless Meetings* (New York, NY: AMACOM, 2013), 5.

2. Christopher Byrne, *Funny Business: Harnessing the Power of Play to Give Your Company a Competitive Advantage* (Wayne, NJ: Career Press, 2015), 77.

CHAPTER 9

1. Saketh Guntupalli and Maryann Karinch, *Sex and Cancer: Intimacy, Romance, and Love After Diagnosis and Treatment* (Lanham, MD: Rowman & Littlefield, 2017).

2. Tim Hains, "Rescued Woman Blows Up On CNN Reporter for Heartless Hurricane Harvey Coverage," CNN, August 29, 2017;

_www.realclearpolitics.com/video/2017/08/29/res-cued_woman_cnn_for_heartless_hurricane_harvey_coverage.html_

3. Piercarlo Valdesolo, "Flattery Will Get You Far," _Scientific American,_ January 12, 2010; _www.scientificamerican.com/article/flattery-will-get-you-far/_

4. Elaine Chan and Jaideep Sengupta, "Insincere Flattery Actually Works: A Dual Attitudes Perspective," _Journal of Marketing Research,_ February 2010, vol. 47, no. 1, 122–133.

5. Piercarlo Valdesolo, "Flattery Will Get You Far."

CHAPTER 10

1. Steven Pinker, "What Our Language Habits Reveal," TEDGlobal 2005; _www.ted.com/talks/steven_pinker_on_language_and_thought/transcript_

2. Alan McKee, "What Is Textual Analysis," _Textual Analysis: A Beginner's Guide_ (London: SAGE Publications, 2003), 1.

3. Ibid., 4.

4. Josef Adalian, "The Most Popular U.S. TV Shows in 18 Countries Around the World," _Vulture,_ December 2, 2015; _www.vulture.com/2015/12/most-popular-us-tv-shows-around-the-world.html_

5. Ibid.

6. "23 Fascinating Words with No Direct English Translations," _Huffington Post,_ December 6, 2017; _www.huffingtonpost.com/2014/02/20/english-translation-words_n_4790396.html_

7. Pinker, "What Our Language Habits Reveal."